Science and Psychology

Science and Psychology provides a comprehensive introduction to the structure and characteristics of scientific explanation, using examples from a variety of sciences to illuminate the scientific approach taken in psychology. In addition, the authors discuss a range of conceptual issues particular to psychology. They examine the concepts of free will, consciousness, and purposeful behaviour, and consider the social implications of possible future changes in our understanding of these concepts and of ourselves. The final chapters of the book provide an account of what psychology can tell us about the history and origins of science.

Assuming no previous understanding of either the philosophy of science or any science other than psychology, *Science and Psychology* is an ideal resource for both final-year undergraduates and postgraduates studying psychology. Psychologists and other scientists who wish to further their understanding of the relationship between psychology and the natural sciences may also find the contents to be of interest.

Richard Wilton has held the posts of Assistant Professor at The University of Texas and Senior Lecturer at The University of Dundee. His interests include animal learning, human learning and memory, and mental problem-solving. Most recently, as a Senior Teaching Fellow, he taught an undergraduate course focusing upon the issues discussed in this book.

Trevor Harley holds the Chair in Cognitive Psychology at the University of Dundee, where he was previously Head of Department and Dean. He is now a science writer and journalist. He completed his undergraduate and postgraduate degrees at the University of Cambridge, and worked for many years on language, mental illness, and consciousness. He is the author of several books, including *The Psychology of Language*, currently in its fourth edition.

Science and Psychology

Richard Wilton and Trevor Harley

Routledge
Taylor & Francis Group

LONDON AND NEW YORK

First published 2018
by Routledge
2 Park Square, Milton Park, Abingdon, Oxon OX14 4RN

and by Routledge
711 Third Avenue, New York, NY 10017

Routledge is an imprint of the Taylor & Francis Group, an informa business

British Library Cataloguing-in-Publication Data
A catalogue record for this book is available from the British Library

Library of Congress Cataloging-in-Publication Data
Names: Wilton, Richard, author. | Harley, Trevor A., author.
Title: Science and psychology / Richard Wilton & Trevor Harley.
Description: Abingdon, Oxon ; New York, NY : Routledge, 2017. |
    Includes bibliographical references.
Identifiers: LCCN 2017002083 | ISBN 9781138693791
    (hardback : alk. paper) | ISBN 9781138693807 (pbk. : alk. paper) |
    ISBN 9781315529295 (ebook : alk. paper)
Subjects: LCSH: Psychology. | Science.
Classification: LCC BF121 .W54 2017 | DDC 150.1—dc23
LC record available at https://lccn.loc.gov/2017002083

ISBN: 978-1-138-69379-1 (hbk)
ISBN: 978-1-138-69380-7 (pbk)
ISBN: 978-1-315-52929-5 (ebk)

Typeset in Akzidenz Grotesk
by Apex CoVantage, LLC
Printed and bound by CPI Group (UK) Ltd, Croydon, CR0 4YY

Contents

Preface

The aim of this book is to acquaint the reader with the general structure of scientific explanation, its application to psychology, some larger questions concerning human beings that may not be open to a scientific resolution, and the contribution that psychology has made to our understanding of scientific progress. It is not a book intended to teach psychology; rather, it is a book *about* psychology – although you may learn some psychology in the course of reading it.

A peculiarity of psychology, as offered for study at universities, is that although psychology is agreed to be a science, the students who take it often have little or no scientific background. Indeed, the data show that the majority of students fall within this category. A premise of this book is that in a number of fundamental respects, the understanding of such students is lacking. For example, students typically are unfamiliar with anything more than a rudimentary knowledge of empirical testing and the criteria that define a good explanation or theory. In Part 1 of the book, these concepts are explained in depth, beginning with the assumption that the reader has no relevant background knowledge outside psychology.

Nevertheless, in the course of this explanation, it soon becomes apparent that, unique within the sciences, additional issues arise within psychology. In Part 2 of the book, some of these issues are examined, such as the question of whether human beings may have free will (and whether this is open to empirical test), and the problems that arise in the attempt to understand consciousness.

Finally, in Part 3, we consider what psychology tells us about the limits of our understanding in science, and whether science (having arisen only once in the entire history of mankind), may be an 'unnatural' activity, when considered in the context of what psychology has shown us about our innately based mental capabilities.

We have made our language gender neutral by choosing 'he' or 'she' at random or using the conventional 'they/their', 'his/her', and 'he or she'.

Much of the work for this book is based on a course of lectures given by the first author at the University of Dundee. We would like to thank Marian Antram and Philip Quinlan for the helpful comments they made during the writing of the book, and Marian Antram, again, for the cover design.

PART 1

The characteristics of scientific explanation and its application to psychology

With some reservations, which will become apparent as we work through this part of the book, it could be said that the aim of science is to describe and explain the world in which we live. In the five chapters of Part 1, we examine, in detail, the characteristics of this process.

Before we begin, however, a comment is in order concerning the scope of the material. Much of the material is derived from work carried out in philosophy; and some of the examples used to illustrate various points are taken from sciences other than psychology, for example, physics. However, the book has been written on the assumption that the reader has no background in either philosophy or these other sciences. In addition, we, the authors, have chosen examples that can be simply explained and that are suitable for use on several different occasions in the book, thereby keeping their number to a minimum. We do not want readers to give up on a task which they might otherwise find interesting, and perhaps revealing, because they lack the relevant background in these areas. So do not feel daunted when you first encounter some philosophical term or an example of some effect from the non-psychological sciences. There are not many of them, and the same ones are used repeatedly throughout the book. The book was written specifically for readers who have a background only in basic psychology (although we hope and believe that even the scientists among you will learn a thing or two about science).

We should note also that, ideally, the book is best read as a novel is read – that is, begun at the beginning and ending at the end. We say this because what is said in most of the chapters (particularly the ones in Part 1 of the book) presumes an understanding of what was said in previous chapters. And, like a good novel, we hope that reading the book will result in an expansion of your horizons.

CHAPTER 1

The defining characteristic of science

In later chapters of this part of the book, we shall discuss in detail the characteristics of scientific explanation, including, for example, theories and laws. However, before we become fully immersed in this, we shall, in this short but essential chapter, focus on the single most important and defining characteristic of science, which is that *any statement made in science must be open to test by observation of the world, thereby enabling one to gather information about its truth or falsity.* Let's see what this means.

Consider the following statement: if you stroke this cat, it will purr. Now, suppose that Jones and Smith differ as to whether they believe the statement is true. All they have to do in order to find out whether it is true or false is stroke the cat and *observe* whether it purrs or not. By saying that they can observe whether or not the cat purrs, we mean they can use their eyes, ears, and other sensory organs or instruments (a microphone perhaps, or a video camera) to determine whether or not the cat purrs. If they observe that it purrs, they have *discovered* that the statement is true; if they observe that it does not purr, they have discovered that it is false.

Not all statements are open to test by observation; hence, to say that a statement is a scientific one is to say something in particular, namely that its truth or falsity can be tested by observation. To illustrate this, consider the following example of a statement that could not be included within science: "It is wrong to keep animals locked up in cages." Here there is no observation that a person can make in order to find out whether this statement is true or false. All anyone can do is say what his or her own beliefs are concerning what is right or wrong, and in that context, say whether they *believe* the statement is true or false. To illustrate: suppose Jones believes it is wrong to keep animals in cages, and Smith believes it is not wrong. This difference in beliefs could obtain even though each of them has made all the observations that could be relevant to what they believe, for example, whether the animal shrieks and scratches at the bars of the cage, and even whether or not they accept that the animal suffers as a result of being caged.

For clarity, note that we are not here denying that the statement "It is wrong to keep animals locked up in cages" is false, and we are not denying that it is true. Rather, we are saying that whether it is true or false cannot be discovered by observation. We might be able to establish its truth or falsity by argument from moral principles, but such an argument would not be a scientific one.

The above should also make us realise that, since not all statements are scientific statements, science cannot tell us everything that we might want to know. For a further illustration of this point, consider a confusion that often occurs in discussion of morality and evolution. Evolution may have made us selfish and aggressive, caring for our own family at the expense of others (say). And because our disposition to behave selfishly and aggressively is a result of evolution, we might say that this is our natural way of behaving. However, to show that it is natural to behave in some particular way implies nothing whatsoever about whether it is morally right to behave in that way. In other words, it may be true that we are disposed to behave in some particular way, and that we can discover that this is so by observation; but in itself, this implies nothing about how we should behave (i.e. nothing about the rightness or wrongness of behaving in this way). Similarly, although some behaviour may be unnatural in that it has not been selected in the process of evolution, this unnaturalness does not imply that it is wrong (and neither does it imply that it is right). Thus, for example, one could believe that homosexual behaviour is unnatural, in the sense described, and also believe there is nothing wrong with it. The morally right way to behave cannot be deduced from any assertion about evolution.

The argument being made here was first put forward by David Hume (an 18th-century philosopher – see Ayer, 1980), who pointed out that one cannot get an "ought" from an "is". That is, one cannot make a deduction as to how one should (ought to) behave from some observation concerning how one is disposed to behave.

Given the preceding discussion, it may be worth noting that some people believe that one can discover the truth or falsity of statements about what is morally right or wrong by a means other than observation, for example, through revelation from God or consultation of a book such as the Bible. This sort of claim is of no concern to us here, since we are concerned only with science, so we will not discuss it further. However, in other contexts – for example, the discussion of various issues concerning comparisons between science and religion – you might find it useful to bear the distinction in mind in order to avoid confusion about what can and cannot be claimed in science.

In a teaching course based on the contents of this book, students were examined upon their ability to answer some questions. The students were given one hour to answer each question, and were not allowed to consult any notes. We thought you, also, might try your hand at answering these questions in order to discover whether you (really) do understand the material. If you are taking a course which uses this book, the course instructor could set and mark your answers. Alternatively, you could write your answer and ask some other person to read it in order to see whether your answer makes sense. We might note also that the perennial advice that lecturers give in answering questions is to read the question carefully and actually try to answer the question as set, rather than some other question which you can readily answer, but unfortunately has not been set! Our procedure, at the end of each chapter, will be to set questions relevant to that chapter.

Having said all this, we have only one question for Chapter 1; our excuse is that the chapter is only a short one. Here is the question.

1   What distinguishes scientific statements from non-scientific statements?

CHAPTER 2

The structure of scientific explanation

The Standard View

In Chapter 1, we said that the aim of science is to describe and explain the world in which we live. Most importantly, within this context, we then said that the hypotheses we might have about the world must be open to test by observation. It is this ability to test hypotheses that distinguishes the scientific enterprise from other attempts to describe and explain the world.

In the remaining chapters of Part 1, we shall engage in a detailed examination of scientific description and explanation. Two different analyses, called the *Standard View* and the *Alternative View*, will be considered. Both views accept the primary importance of statements being open to test by observation, and also have much else in common. However, as we shall see, the two analyses differ in one fundamental respect and, in consequence, have very different implications for what can be claimed in science.

Before we do this, however, it is necessary to introduce some technical concepts which should assist our understanding throughout the book. It is essential for you to become sufficiently familiar with these so that you can wield them readily without too much thought. They are commonly used in the philosophical literature, and we believe them to be invaluable in our own presentation.

The first of these concepts is simple and has already been used. It concerns the definition of a *statement*. A statement (e.g. "John loves Mary") is either true or false; by contrast, a meaningless concatenation of words (e.g. "loves, Mary, John") is neither true nor false: in this case, the concepts of true and false are inapplicable.

The second concept concerns the meaning of the term '*implies*'. The meaning of 'implies' can be illustrated as follows: suppose A implies B. This means that if A is true, then B is true. That is, it would be a contradiction to suppose that A is true and B is false. Here are a couple of examples. The statement "All swans are white" implies that "This swan is white". "John is a father" implies "John has a child". Another way of saying that A implies B is to say that B can be deduced from A. Thus, if all swans are white, we can deduce that "This swan is white". The words 'implies' and 'deduce' are both frequently used in the literature. Note that "A implies B" does not mean that B implies A ("All swans are white" means that if this thing is a swan, then it is white, not that all white things are swans).

A mistake easily made is to confuse the use of the term 'inference' with that of 'deduction'. Suppose Robinson Crusoe discovers a depression in the sand that looks like a human footprint. And, perhaps because it is likely to have been caused by a human foot, he may infer that it was caused by a human foot. However, this does not mean that he has thereby deduced that it was caused by a human foot – for it is possible that it was caused by something else (for example, it may have been produced by the wind). Thus, to infer that something is the case is not to deduce that it is the case. Rather, it is simply to make an educated guess that it is so. Inference does not have the same meaning as deduction or implication. As a test of your understanding of the difference, ask yourself whether Sherlock Holmes actually did deduce (rather than infer) all that he was said to deduce.

THE STANDARD VIEW

Now let's return to our consideration of the Standard and Alternative Views of description and explanation in science. We shall consider the Standard View first. Then we will argue that the Standard View is actually incorrect, and this conclusion will lead us to a consideration of the Alternative View. You might ask: why bother even to consider the Standard View, given that it is wrong? One reason is that many scientists and laypersons believe the Standard View to be correct, and on this basis, they incorrectly accept arguments, which appear to be convincing, about the degree to which we can be certain about the statements made in science; it is best to be aware of such errors in reading and listening to what others say about science. Another reason is that one must understand the Standard View in order to fully appreciate the different profound implications of the Alternative View. And yet another reason is that much of what will be said in this chapter applies also to the Alternative View, so do not skip it on the grounds that eventually we shall decide that the Standard View is wrong.

According to the Standard View (Bechtel, 1988, pp. 1–70; Hempel, 1966, Chapter 5; Nagel, 1961, Chapter 6), science consists of a body of known facts and the explanation of these. The known facts are described by what are called observation statements, and any explanation of these facts is expressed in statements which postulate laws and theories. Let's consider the three kinds of statement in detail.

OBSERVATION STATEMENTS

Suppose we want to find out whether some individual object has some particular property. For example, suppose we want to know the colour of the swan that lives on our village pond. We go down to the pond, observe the swan and its colour, and write down the result of our observation – "The swan on the village pond is white" – in our notebook. What we have written down is called an observation statement. An observation statement is a statement that describes the result of an observation. It makes an assertion about some particular observed entity, such as the swan on the village pond. Another example would be "The poker by my fireplace is one metre in length". A third example would be "The red billiard ball is five feet from the white billiard ball".

It should be noted that the assertion made by the observation statement does not describe a *defining* characteristic of the object we are talking about. If it did, we would not have to make an *observation* in order to make the assertion. Rather, the statement reports a genuine *discovery* about the world. One observes the swan (defined, say, by its size and shape or whatever), which, as far as anyone knows before making the observation, could be either white or not white, and discovers that it is white. We do not need to go to the village pond in order to be able to write down "A swan is a bird".

Contrary to what we have supposed, some readers might suggest that a swan is white by definition, and so could not be not-white. But, if so, then rather than argue about whether they are right or wrong in making this claim, we would simply avoid using "This swan is white" as an example of an observation statement – just as we would not use the example "This husband is married". There is, we think, no need to discuss this further, for we believe it would be a diversion to do so in the present context. As should be clear, what we are concerned with, at present, is making and reporting discoveries about the world.

Supposedly, any observation statement is *incorrigible*, which means that its truth is not open to doubt. Put another way, the statement always constitutes a faithful record of what one has observed. Thus, it is supposed that an observation statement cannot later be shown to be false by reference to any other discovery one might make. As will shortly become apparent, according to the Standard View, this characteristic of observation statements is one of great importance.

Consistent with what has been said above, in daily life we often speak of facts as states of affairs which can be stated independently of any interpretation (explanation) of them. "Just give me the facts" we say. Hence, as should be apparent, observation statements are, according to the Standard View, statements of fact. It is often said that scientists like to express their findings in terms of facts. Then everyone can agree on 'what is' and then perhaps argue about what laws or theories might explain the facts.

Now, continuing with the Standard View, let us examine the two kinds of statement (ones that express laws and theories) that are used to explain the facts. As we shall see, an important characteristic of both these kinds of statement is that they go beyond the observed facts in that they might be shown to be false by observations not yet made. Neither of these two kinds of statement can therefore be demonstrated to be true: they are not incorrigible.

STATEMENTS THAT ASSERT LAWS

A statement of a particular law asserts that all the observable entities of a particular kind (whatever their location in space and time) have a particular property. For example, "All swans are white" is a possible law. Laws are usually formulated by scientists in the following manner: the scientist makes one or more observations of individual entities (e.g. one swan being white, then another, then another, and so on), and then generalises from these cases to make the claim "All swans are white." It is sometimes thought that more than one observation must be made in order to formulate a law, but this is not so. Although it would be very unusual (for reasons we need not enter into here), a scientist might propose a law based upon one single observation. And in this context, note that however many instances have been observed with the same result (be it just one or one million), a generalisation to even more unobserved cases is implied when a law is postulated. This implication follows because the concept 'all' implies the truth of an infinite number of statements, each referring to some different individual entity.

A law is proposed to explain observations in the low-level sense that the observation(s) can be deduced from the law. Hence, from the law that all swans are white, one can deduce (explain) the fact that the swan on the village pond is white.

Testing laws

As explained previously in our discussion of incorrigibility, any statement about an individual entity implied by a supposed law can be tested by observation and perhaps shown to be true. But however many individual cases are shown to be true, it does not mean that the law has been shown to be true. For, as should be clear, the fact that a law refers to an infinite number of cases implies that some of these cases will forever remain untested. Therefore, the law itself cannot be shown to be true.

So, given that a law cannot be shown to be true, how could a test be made to determine its truth or falsity? Well, as Popper, a notable philosopher of science, pointed out in 1959, a proposed law may be shown to be false (if it is false). One could make a single observation which results in an observation statement that contradicts the law. For example, one may observe a black swan on the pond further down the lane, and so write down the observation statement "This swan is black". Hence, given the truth of such an observation statement, the proposed law "All swans are white" must be false. So we can, by observation, discover something about whether our supposed law is true or false: if we have tested the law a number of times and in each case discovered that the relevant swan is white, we can continue to believe that the law is true, whilst recognising the possibility that in later tests, it may be shown to be false.

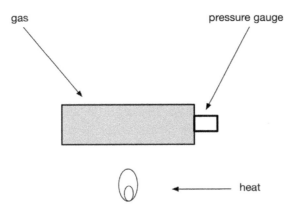

Figure 2.1 Apparatus used to demonstrate Boyle's law.

Now, for illustration, let's consider a classic example of a law. Suppose a gas is contained within an enclosed chamber (see Figure 2.1). Boyle's law states that if the temperature of the gas is increased, then the pressure exerted by the gas on the walls of the chamber will increase. This can be expressed as:

Pressure is proportional to Temperature.

The law can be tested by taking any one single instance of a gas, heating it, and observing any change in pressure exerted on the wall of the chamber. An increase in pressure would be consistent with the law, and so we could continue to believe that the law is true. And, by contrast, no change in pressure, or a decrease, would show the law to be false. So far, in the history of science, there has been no falsifying instance, and so most scientists (probably all) continue to believe that the law is true.

Another classic example of a law is Newton's law of gravitation. This states that any body is attracted to any other body with a gravitational force that depends on the masses of the two bodies and their distance apart.

In attempting to understand Newton's law, the reader may ask what is meant by the term 'mass' of a body. The meaning is not easy to explain, and so we will give you a simple definition which is actually incorrect, but which we believe is not misleading for non-physicists. For the term 'mass', you can substitute 'weight'. As shown in the equation below, the greater the masses of the two bodies (their masses being designated by M_1 and M_2), the greater is the attraction between them; and the greater the distance between them (D), the less the attraction between them.

The force of attraction between the two masses is proportional to $M_1 \times M_2$ divided by D^2.

In this equation, D^2 means $D \times D$ (i.e. D squared). Therefore, for example, if the distance between the two bodies were 5 miles, then the attraction between them would be $M_1 \times M_2$ divided by 25, whereas if the distance were 10 miles, it would be $M_1 \times M_2$ divided by 100.

The most familiar case of gravitational attraction is that of an apple supposedly falling from a tree upon Newton's head. As Newton realised, the apple fell because of the gravitational force between it (M_1) and the earth (M_2). Another case, less commonly considered, is that between two billiard balls on a table. This case is less obvious because the billiard balls do not move towards each other (unless one of them is struck by a cue). Why is this? According to Newton, there must be a gravitational attraction between them. The answer is that indeed there is, but their masses are relatively small (unlike the earth in the case of the apple falling to the earth), and the little attraction between them that does obtain is countered by friction from the table. If there were no friction – as would be the case if the balls were located in otherwise empty space, where nothing else had any effect on them – the balls would move towards each other until they met.

We have chosen Boyle's law and Newton's law of gravitation as examples because we will refer to them again in later discussion. So remember them. Some examples of laws in psychology are: the Gestalt laws of perception, the capacity of a person's short-term memory is seven plus or minus two items, the laws concerning proactive and retroactive interference in memory, the laws concerning cognitive dissonance, and Weber's Law describing how we detect changes in stimuli.

THEORETICAL STATEMENTS

The statements of a theory contain terms which, although they may refer to entities of some sort (e.g. electrons or logogens), do not necessarily refer to entities that can be observed. Hence, they differ from observation statements and laws. Consider, for example, kinetic theory, formulated by Kelvin in the 19th century (see Hempel, 1966, p. 73). Kinetic theory states that any gas consists of many small particles, each too small to be detected individually, moving about randomly (see Figure 2.1). Theories explain laws and observations. For example, kinetic theory explains Boyle's law, and all its implied individual observations, in the following way. When the gas is heated, the speed of each particle increases. Hence, the number of particles striking the wall at any one time increases, thereby increasing the measured pressure. We have chosen this theory as an example because it will be useful in later discussion.

Testing theories

We have seen that the entities to which theoretical statements refer may be unobservable. In kinetic theory, for example, the pressure exerted on the wall of the chamber by any single particle cannot be measured: the particle is too small to be detected individually and its pressure is too slight. We don't have access to a single particle. So, the properties of a single particle have no implications for observation. Hence, the question arises as to how the theory can be tested by observation. The answer has already been given in the preceding paragraph: the theory makes the observable prediction that when the gas is heated, the pressure on the walls of the chamber will increase.

It may be useful to describe this testing procedure in more general terms, in order that it becomes clear how it could be used in other cases, whatever the subject matter and theory. We would begin by manipulating what psychologists call an independent variable – something we change, such as heating, in the case of Boyle's law, in order to see whether it has an effect on some dependent variable. The particular independent variable chosen is one that, according to the theory, has an effect on the unobserved entities postulated (e.g. very small particles). And, in turn, the consequences of this effect (e.g. increasing the velocity of the particles) are predicted to have an effect on the observable dependent variable (e.g. the reading given on a pressure gauge). If the predicted effect occurs, we can continue to believe that the theory is true. If it does not occur, then we should conclude that the theory must be false.

One example from psychology is exhibited by the testing of Morton's (1969) logogen theory. You can think of a logogen as a simple internal mechanism which accumulates evidence for the occurrence of a word when an auditory or visual input is presented to a subject. A variety of independent variables, such as the frequency with which a particular word generally occurs in the language, is assumed to affect the state of an unobserved logogen. And, in turn, the state of a logogen determines the state of the dependent variable, this latter being the response of a person when, for example, they are asked to say what word was presented.

An additional point to note is that in many theories, the theoretical entities also affect each other. For example, according to logogen theory, a logogen is affected by the contents of semantic memory as well as the present external input. This multiple determination makes any calculation of effects on dependent variables more complicated. But this is of no great consequence, for since the content of semantic memory is determined by previous inputs, the theory can still be tested by deducing the outcome of a causal chain from independent to dependent variables, as previously described.

You might find it useful here to note that the package consisting of kinetic theory, the laws it implies (e.g. Boyle's law), and the individual states of the world implied by the law (e.g. the behaviour of a particular gas on a particular occasion) constitutes a good illustrative example of the relations between theories, laws, observations, and testing – and so can be helpful in reminding one of these relations. The theory implies the laws, and the laws imply the occurrence of particular states of affairs. An observation can then be made to discover whether a particular state actually does obtain. And, following this, the observation statement can be compared with the corresponding statement deduced from the theory. If the two statements match, we can continue to believe that the theory and law are true; if they do not match, the theory and law must be false.

More on testing theories

We have seen that a theory can be tested in that it makes predictions about observables. And we have seen that when the predictions are not confirmed, we can conclude that the theory is false. Also, we have seen that when the theory correctly predicts an event, we can continue to believe it is true. But, in this latter case, can we say further that the theory has been proved to be true? The answer is no. We cannot say the theory has been proved because it is always logically possible that although the theory may explain some data (e.g. the confirmed predictions), some other theory could also explain those data (even if nobody has ever thought of it). Hence, although the theory implies the data, the reverse is not true (see Hempel, 1966, pp. 6–8): the occurrence of the data does not imply that the theory is true. The following example should make this argument clear.

Suppose Theory A implies observation statement O_1. For example, kinetic theory implies that an increase in temperature increases the speed of the particles, thereby bringing about a greater frequency of hits on the chamber wall, and therefore an increase in measured pressure.

Now suppose that Theory B also implies observation statement O_1. For example, suppose that Smith has a theory which implies that an increase in temperature increases the weight of each particle, resulting in each particle striking the chamber wall with greater force, resulting thereby in greater pressure. Therefore, observation statement O_1 does not imply Theory A as it is also compatible with Theory B.

Thus, even if we accept that observation statements are incorrigible, we cannot deduce that some particular theory which explains those observations is true. Therefore, the truth of any theoretical statement is always open to doubt. Of course, as noted above, we can continue to believe the theory if we so wish; but that does not mean the theory is true. In relation to the illustration given above, Kelvin might still believe that kinetic theory (A) is true and Smith might still believe that her theory (B) is true.

We should perhaps mention that there is also another reason why a theory can never be shown to be true. A theory usually (perhaps always, we are not sure) implies laws. For example, kinetic theory implies Boyle's law. Therefore, since we cannot show a law to be true (because it is impossible to make an infinite number of observations), we cannot show that a theory which implies that law is true. Note that this reason for concluding that a theory cannot be proven to be true differs from, and is independent of, the previously given reason that refers to the possibility of some other theory also making the relevant predictions. You can readily appreciate this by noting that even if we could make the infinite number of observations that showed a law to be true (e.g. Boyle's law), there would still be some other theory, in addition to kinetic theory, which could account for that law. With respect to understanding the overall characteristics of explanation in science, we think that in the present context, the inability to prove a law is of minor interest, and this is why we include it only as an afterthought. Our major point is that some alternative theory is always possible and it may be the one that is true.

Given that a theory can be shown to be false, we shall now consider a further point. Any one theory usually consists of more than one statement. For example, kinetic theory includes statements about the velocity, weight, and elasticity of the assumed particles. In psychology, the same applies for logogen theory in that it refers both to environmental and semantic input. Another good example is given by atomic theory. It is common knowledge that, according to atomic theory, matter consists of atoms. At the centre of the atom lies a nucleus consisting of a neutron and a proton, and circling round the nucleus are a number of electrons. Such an atomic structure can be used to explain all the observable properties of matter, for example, why sugar dissolves in water. Now let us suppose, for the sake of argument, that atomic theory made a prediction that was shown to be false. What particular statement within the theory is in error? The answer is that one cannot say – for the prediction of any one observation depends on the way all the supposed constituents of the atom interact with each other. And it could be any one, or more, of these interactions that are incorrectly specified in the theory. In other words, when a theory has been shown to be false, all that we know is that it is false in at least one respect – we may not know exactly where the fault or faults lie. This conclusion may seem disappointing (and perhaps it is), but nevertheless, the theory has been shown to be false; and it is then open to scientists either to discard the theory entirely or to modify it in those respects they believe to be false, and then to carry out tests of the modified theory, just as they would in the case of any other theory.

Our overall conclusion then is that theories can be tested. Although it is not possible to prove a theory (show it to be true), it can be shown to be false (if it is false). As in the case of laws, the theory might be shown to be false by one single observation.

Criteria used in deciding between theories

Earlier, we saw that two or more different theories can predict some facts in common. How then can the decision be made as to which of the two theories to adopt? According to the Standard View, the matter is obvious and straightforward. Although the two theories may predict some facts in common, they may not predict all in common. For example, consider again Smith's alternative to kinetic theory described previously, which asserts that heat increases the weight of the particles. Like kinetic theory, it predicts an increase in pressure on the walls of the chamber, but would also predict that if the gas were to be weighed, its weight would have increased. And, by contrast, kinetic theory predicts no increase in weight. Hence, we could weigh the heated gas and if there were no increase in weight, reject Smith's theory, declaring it false because the result is inconsistent with it.

Why do we say, given the Standard View, that in order to select between two theories, it is obvious that we should use the criterion of rejecting the false theory? The answer is obvious! Our goal in science is to discover how the world works. Falsification tells us that the world does not work in a particular way. Therefore, we reject the falsified theory, justifying this as serving to advance our goal. For illustrative contrast, someone might suggest that we should reject a theory on grounds related to the nationality of the person who proposed the theory; but surely the adoption of such a criterion could not be justified given our goal in science. Hence, we would find it unacceptable.

A classic example in the history of science can be used to illustrate the use of falsification as a criterion of rejection. (For details, see Butterfield, 1957, Chapter 11, pp. 206–221; or Conant, 1951, Chapter 7.) Consider the effect of heat on various metals in our normal atmosphere. Suppose that heating a particular metal results in the production of a red powder. In the 17th century, this observation would have been explained by some scientists by reference to an inferred theoretical substance called phlogiston. Phlogiston was presumed to be a component of all metals, such that when the metal was heated, the phlogiston was driven from it, with only the powder remaining. Alternatively, according to the competing theory, the production of the powder could be explained by reference to an inferred substance called oxygen. Oxygen was presumed to be a gaseous component of the atmosphere which, when a metal was heated, combined with the metal to produce the powder. Thus, the two theories explained the basic effect of combustion (burning) in very different ways. Nevertheless, the theories can be empirically (i.e. observationally) differentiated, in that phlogiston theory predicts that, since phlogiston has been lost, the red powder left after burning will weigh less than the original unheated metal. By contrast, oxygen theory predicts that, following the combination of the metal with oxygen, the red powder will weigh more than the original unheated metal. Empirical tests (i.e. observation) carried out in the 18th century showed that the red powder weighed more than the original metal, and therefore phlogiston theory was discarded.

Now let's consider an example from psychology. We have chosen this example because two fundamentally different theories were compared, each having a wide range of application. Moreover, an understanding of each will be of relevance in reading later chapters of this book.

In general, human beings and other animals come to behave adaptively to their environment by a process of learning. Hence, as might be expected, the study of learning has always been a significant area of research in psychology. We shall consider here two competing theories concerning the processes which account for learned behaviour. In their most basic form, they were first contrasted in the first half of the 20th century, and it is these basic versions with which we shall be concerned. According to stimulus-response (S-R) theory, the movements that an animal first makes, following its birth, are random. Hence, initially the animal is no more likely to exhibit an adaptive response (e.g. one that results in attaining food) than not. However, if in some particular situation (call it a stimulus), one of these random movements happens to be followed by a reinforcer, such as food, then a connection is formed between that stimulus and the response, forming an S-R unit. The connection between the two is such that if on any subsequent occasion the animal again encounters that stimulus (or a very similar one), the probability of it making that same movement is increased. Thus, the animal's behaviour becomes adapted to its environment in that, generally speaking, if some particular sequence of movements in some particular situation is followed by the 'delivery' of food on one occasion, it is likely that that those same movements will yield food on subsequent occasions. According to S-R theory, all learning is of this sort. For example, the theory accounts for the following finding. Suppose a hungry rat is placed in the start box of a straight runway which has food at its end. On the first occasion when the rat is placed in the runway, it will merely 'amble' randomly along the runway (the rat can neither smell nor see the food) until eventually it arrives, by chance, at the food cup and eats the food. Such trials are then repeated, for example, once a day. And since any random forward movements that may occasionally occur are strongly reinforced because they more immediately result in the ingestion (eating) of the food, the rat will, after a number of trials, emit only forward movements; and so the time taken for the animal to traverse the runway decreases. Note that the increase in speed does not occur because the animal comes to anticipate food. Rather, it occurs because those S-R chains that happen to lead most directly to food get strengthened, and so eventually they are the only ones that occur. No other process is involved: no thinking, no anticipation of the food – just S-R chains.

This simple theory also explains more complex behaviours. For example, it explains how rats learn to run a maze. Suppose we have a T-shaped maze with food on the left-hand side and no food on the right-hand side. The rat is placed at the start of the maze (the 'bottom' of the T) for the first time. It may then randomly make a sequence of movements that results in its arrival at the crosspiece of the T, and at that point makes some movement that takes it to the right or left. Suppose the rat's turn is to the right. This response is not reinforced since there is no food; hence the response of turning right is not strengthened, and the rat learns nothing – no S-R chain has been established. Now, by contrast, suppose that on some trial (any trial) the animal happens to make a turn to the left. The connection of this response to the stimulus of being at the crosspiece will then be strengthened because it is followed by food; and therefore, it is more likely to occur again on the next trial. Hence, over a number of trials, the turning-left response will get stronger and stronger so that eventually the rat turns left on every trial.

It may be noted here that one can see the potentially very wide application of this theory to the explanation of all learned behaviour, in that all such behaviour, no matter how seemingly complex, might be reduced to sequences of taking a turn in one direction rather than another. One might argue that the theory has one of the characteristics of a good theory in that it has the potential to explain much by means of very simple processes (but more of that in a later chapter!).

Now compare S-R theory with an alternative account of learning. According to Tolman (1948), when the animal is placed in either the runway or the maze and randomly moves about on the initial trials, it picks up information about the layout of its surroundings; and this information is stored in a cognitive map. In general, a cognitive map is a representation of whatever environment has been encountered by the animal. In the present case, the information stored on the "map" corresponds to the structure of the runway or maze, rather as a map of the London Underground corresponds to the actual London Underground. Given the formation of the cognitive map, the animal's behaviour is explained as follows. When, after some initial experience in the maze, sufficient information has been processed and stored on the map, the animal is again placed at the starting point in the apparatus, it "consults" the cognitive map to determine "what-leads-to-what" (as Tolman put it) in the actual maze. Then, on the basis of this stored information, it makes whatever movements are appropriate to get to the location where food was previously found. In a sense, it anticipates what lies ahead and then acts on the basis of this anticipation.

Now let's see how a test might discriminate between the two theories, such that we could rule one of them out. The following is a simplified and somewhat schematic description of an ingenious experiment carried out by Deutsch and Clarkson (1959). These experimenters constructed a maze which had three alternative routes leading from the start box (see Figure 2.2). Two of these were short and terminated in the same food chamber – shown on the left-hand side of the figure. The other was long and terminated in a different food chamber – shown on the right-hand side of the figure. As shown in the figure, each route could be blocked just beyond the start box. Following preliminary training with food in both chambers, two test trials were carried out. In one of these trials, one of the short routes was blocked just beyond the start box. The result was that upon reaching the block and then being returned to the start box, most of the rats then went down the other short route. On the other test trial, no food was placed in the food chamber common to the two short routes. In this case, upon being returned to the start box, the animal then went down the longer route, the one terminating in the food chamber shown on the right of the figure. This behaviour was exactly the result predicted by the theory that asserts that the animal consults a cognitive map when in the start box. For, in showing what-leads-to-what, the map would indicate that in the blocked case there would, nevertheless, presumably be food in the left-hand side chamber. Hence, upon being returned to the start box, the animal would then go down the other short route terminating in that same food chamber. On the other hand, in the case when there was no block but no food was present in the left-hand side

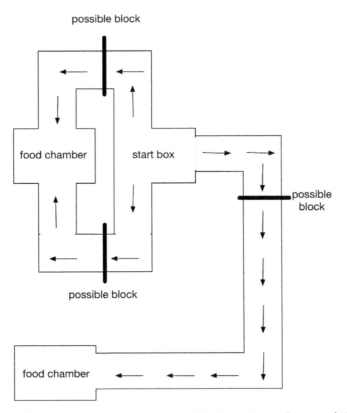

Figure 2.2 Schematic diagram of maze used by Deutsch and Clarkson (1959) to demonstrate the use of a cognitive map in rats.

chamber, the cognitive map would indicate that the alternative short route would not yield food. Hence, upon being returned to the start box, the rat would take the longer route to the right-hand side chamber.

Now let's consider what basic S-R theory predicts. During preliminary training, a chain of S-R connections would have been established along each route, since each would have been reinforced by the ingestion of food in the relevant goal box. These chains are depicted in Figure 2.2 by arrows. Note that, since during training the reinforcer followed a longer sequence of S-R 'units', corresponding to the greater length of the long route, the connective bond linking the start box to an initial movement at the beginning of that route would be weaker than the analogous bond at the beginning of each short route. Now consider the test trials. When one of the short routes failed to result in food, either by blocking or by there being no food in the food chamber, the preceding S-R connections would be weakened (in a process known as extinction) by virtue of having occurred and not having been followed by reinforcement. Therefore, upon being returned to the start box, the animal would take one of the other routes. To simplify somewhat, the animal should take the other short route, since the bond between the stimulus of the start box and the movement that constitutes an entry to that route would be stronger than that between the start box and the movement that would constitute an entry to the longer route. However, as we have seen, it did not always take the other short route. Rather, the route actually taken depended upon whether access to food was prevented by a blockage or by there being no food in the food chamber common to the two short routes. We have here simplified this description somewhat to make it clear that the critical difference between the theories is that Tolman postulates an anticipation of what is to come, based on a consultation of the cognitive map, whereas S-R theory assumes a solely local responding at each point in the maze, with no anticipation.

Having considered the preceding two examples, one from physics and one from psychology, we can say in summary that although different theories often predict many of the same facts, they typically differ in their predictions of other facts. Hence, by testing we can eliminate one of the theories, declaring it to be false.

Note that, as you should already appreciate from previous discussion, what has been said here does not imply that the non-rejected theory is true, for someone else might formulate a third theory which also predicts all the known facts. This formulation of alternative theories may continue with a continuous testing of any two, because however many facts we gather, there may always be a difference in some prediction not yet tested that would enable the scientist to reject one of the theories.

In later chapters, we shall refer again to Tolman and S-R theory. For example, in the case of Tolman, we shall see (in Chapter 8) that the idea that a cognitive map is formed within the brain is again seen to be of considerable significance, in that it enables one to address some problematic issues pertaining to explanations of behaviour that refer to purpose or intentionality.

All that has been said above implies a common view as to what constitutes scientific progress, regardless of what the particular science happens to be – for example, physics, chemistry, biology, or psychology. According to the Standard View, progress is made by eliminating theories about the world that are inconsistent with our present knowledge (observation statements). In this sense, it can be argued, we get nearer to the truth – by eliminating some of the false possibilities.

Finally in this chapter, it is worth noting two points of which you should be aware, even though we shall not discuss either at length. The first is as follows. In response to what has been said concerning the possibility that more than one theory might account for the same set of observations, it might be suggested that there could be two different theories which imply exactly the same set of observations, and hence that no test could be made that differentiated them (Poincaré, 1952). In such a case, other criteria would have to be used for choosing between the theories. However, for the present, note that such criteria are relatively unimportant given the Standard View. The reason they are relatively unimportant is that, presumably, there will actually be very few cases when exactly the same set of observation statements can be deduced, and so very few cases when we cannot rule out one of two competing theories as false. In practice then, according to the Standard View, we shall rarely, if ever, have recourse to criteria other than falsification by the facts.

The second point of which you should be aware is as follows. In order for a theory or law to be open to test by observation, it must imply not only that various states of the world will obtain, but also that others will not. To appreciate this point, consider a theory which does not satisfy this condition. Suppose a theory enables one to deduce only that "Either X will occur or not-X will occur". This theory fails to rule out the occurrence of any possible event. In such a case, the theory makes a claim about the world that must be true. Therefore, any observation we make tells us nothing about the truth or falsity of the theory that we did not know already without making that observation. In this sense, the theory is empty. Note also that as the theory rules nothing out, it has no practical application with respect to enabling us to manipulate or control events in the world. What possible practical use could there be for a theory which says only that, for any possible event X, if you do Y then either X or not-X will occur? Answer, none: the theory provides no guidance whatsoever as to what one should do in order to bring about any particular future state of affairs.

There is, according to some psychologists, a classic example of this kind of theory in psychology. According to them, one can, in Freud's theory, 'deduce' both X and not-X as an outcome in some given situation. For example, Freud might predict that in situation Y, behaviour X will occur; but by the process known as reaction formation, he can also predict that it will not occur. If this is so, then Freud's theory cannot be tested. For this reason, some psychologists do not think it worth including in a psychology degree programme.

Test your understanding of Chapter 2

1   The Standard View of science asserts that science includes three kinds of statement: observation statements, laws, and theories. Describe these and explain how they differ.
2   Describe and explain the rationale that underlies Popper's tenet that scientific theories should be capable of being falsified. Focusing on particular cases, discuss the extent to which theories in psychology conform to this tenet.
3   State the argument that observation statements are incorrigible. Assuming that they are incorrigible, briefly describe the consequent implications with respect to what criteria might be used in selecting between competing theories.

CHAPTER 3

The structure of scientific explanation

The Alternative View

Like the Standard View of science, the Alternative View sees understanding as consisting of statements that describe observations, and express theories and laws. However, it differs in its claim concerning the characteristics of observation statements. As we have seen, according to the Standard View, observation statements are incorrigible (not open to doubt). Such statements supposedly describe a bedrock of facts which can be used to test laws and theories, with the possibility of rendering them false. By contrast, the Alternative View, advocated originally by Duhem in 1904 (see Duhem, 1954; Hesse, 1974; Quine, 1951), differs in the following respects. According to the Alternative View, observation statements are not incorrigible, and therefore there is no bedrock of unassailable statements which a theory, or set of laws, is required to explain. Thus, the Alternative View argues that there is no distinction between statements on the grounds of whether they are incorrigible or not, for no statement is incorrigible. We shall now examine the Alternative View and will argue that it is correct. At times the argument may seem rather abstract; but as we continue to work through these Part 1 chapters, we shall see that the Alternative View has implications that differ profoundly from the Standard View; and we shall provide several examples to show that these have been, and are, of practical relevance in science. Let's consider the Alternative View under the three subheadings we used to explain the Standard View: the structure of scientific explanation, testing, and deciding between alternative theories.

THE STRUCTURE OF SCIENTIFIC EXPLANATION

As already noted, the Alternative View, like the Standard View, asserts that science consists of a body of statements concerning observations, laws, and theories. However, very importantly (you should come to see the importance as we progress), it denies that observation statements are incorrigible.

An advocate of the Standard View might interject at this point and say: Well, it is true that we might make an observation, and write down a statement that we believe is a faithful recording of what we have observed, and yet sometimes, inadvertently, make the error of including within it some interpretation that actually goes beyond what we observed. For example, at dawn, a non-scientific person might report that "The sun is rising above the earth", thinking that they are reporting only what they see and nothing more. However, this statement implies that it is the sun that is moving (rising), and so goes beyond what is actually observed (an increase in spatial separation between the sun and the earth's horizon). Hence, it is not actually an observation statement; for according to the Standard View, what is observed can and should be expressed without interpretation. (A former student of ours thought of this example.) Nevertheless, the advocate of the Standard View says it is always possible to eliminate such interpretation by redescribing what was observed. For example, in the present case, the correct observation statement would be "At dawn there was an increase in spatial separation between the sun and the earth's horizon". This statement appears to be free of interpretation, in that there is no implication of whether it was the sun or the earth that was moving. Thus, the advocate of the Standard View still insists that, provided we are careful to ensure that we do not go beyond reporting what we actually observe, we can write down reports that are incorrigible.

However, according to the Alternative View, what we write down (an observation statement) is nevertheless always open to doubt, for although statements such as the one above can be replaced by some other statement which seems to be incorrigible, there will always remain some interpretation (a going beyond what is observed).

To illustrate this claim, let's begin with what seems to be a far-fetched case, but nevertheless one which actually occurred in the history of science.

In the 19th century, two fundamental assumptions lay at the root of all physics (i.e. how the universe supposedly works). We cannot explain here why these were fundamental, so we ask you, the reader, simply to accept that they were so.

The first assumption was that the whole of space is filled with a substance called the ether – rather as a tank may be filled with water (see Figure 3.1). The second assumption was that the movement of light through space (and therefore through the ether) is similar to the movement of a wave through water – as, for example, when a stone is dropped into a pond and ripples move out from the point at which the stone hit the water.

A third assumption, perhaps less fundamental, but one which would seem hard to deny, was that the earth moves through space (the ether) at a constant speed around the sun.

Let's collectively call these three assumptions, prevailing at the end of the 19th century, the accepted theory. The theory was tested by an experiment carried out by Michelson and Morley in 1887. We shall describe a simplified version of it (see Sklar, 1976, pp. 245–250, for a complete description). As depicted in Figure 3.1, these experimenters measured a distance x (say, for illustration, 100 metres) in a direction parallel to the movement of the earth as it travelled through space (around the sun). A beam of light was then shone from one end of the distance to the other, in the direction taken by the earth. The prediction was the light beam would reach the other end of

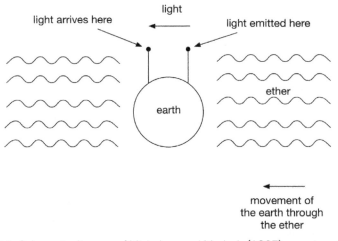

Figure 3.1   Schematic diagram of Michelson and Morley's (1887) experiment.

the distance at a time later than would be the case if the earth were motionless. (By analogy, if a person in a moving boat were to drop a stone from the rear of the boat, the ripples would reach the front of the boat later than if the boat were motionless – because the boat/earth moves ahead of the ripple/light beam.) However, what actually happened was that the time was shorter than expected. That is, the observation statement was that the time taken for the light to travel x distance was y seconds, where the value of y was less than predicted. In fact, the time recorded was identical to that which would be predicted if the earth were not moving at all through space (the ether). Hence, the theory seemed to be false; that is, it seemed that at least one of the three assumptions made above must be false.

But how did physicists respond to this? Lorentz and Fitzgerald (two theoretical physicists) pointed out that the theory could be maintained if the following were true. Suppose, they said, that when any object (for example, a metre stick) moves through space, it contracts (becomes shorter) along the direction in which it is moving. This proposal has the following implication for the Michelson and Morley experiment. When the metre stick was, for the purpose of measuring out the distance x prior to the start of the experiment, aligned parallel with the movement of the earth, it contracted. It contracted because, being an object on the earth, it was then moving in the same direction as the earth. Therefore, the stick was then actually less than one metre in length, and so the distance measured for the light to travel was less than x metres. Therefore, consistent with the theory, the time taken by the light to travel the distance was shorter than it would have been had the distance actually been x metres. So what we have here is an observation statement: "The time taken for the light to travel x metres was y seconds". And we have a theory which, given this supposed incorrigible fact, makes a prediction that is refuted. However, rather than giving up the theory, the theorists proposed that the observation statement was false! That is, the observation statement should have been: "The time taken for the light to travel z metres (where z was less than x) was y seconds".

GENERAL CONCLUSION

The seeming discovery of some fact in the world by the use of a measuring instrument depends upon other assumed facts about the world. For example, in the case of the Michelson and Morley experiment, the correct determination of the distance the light had to travel, using a measuring rod, depends on the truth of the assumption that objects do not contract when they are moving. Such an assumption is often called an auxiliary or background assumption, because it is one of the innumerable beliefs we have about the world that we don't usually even realise we hold and would therefore ordinarily not even query. (You, the reader, would agree, we hope, that this particular assumption is one such belief.) Fitzgerald (1889) and Lorentz (1892) pointed out that if this auxiliary assumption were false, then the theory need not be rejected, since the contradiction between the prediction from the theory and the observation statement could be resolved by concluding that the observation statement, rather than the theory, was false. Shortly, we shall see that the sort of reasoning we have seen employed in relation to the Michelson and Morley experiment applies generally: that is, no observation statement is merely a faithful recording of what it is that is observed, for its truth depends on the truth of any number of other (auxiliary) assumptions. In other words, observation statements are not incorrigible: their truth is always open to doubt. Thus, just as in the case of the Michelson and Morley experiment, it is possible always to preserve one's belief that a theory is true by denying the truth of an observation statement that apparently refutes that theory.

To conclude this description of the Michelson and Morley experiment, three comments might be in order. First, the reader may care to note the following clarification. The point being made here is not one that merely concerns the accuracy of measurement, such that perhaps the only problem was that the measuring instrument may not have been manufactured to as precise a specification as it should have been, or that the experimenters were sloppy in taking the measure. Rather, it concerns some law of nature which is assumed to be true, but in fact is false (e.g. bodies do not change in length according to their velocity). However, having said this, perhaps assumptions concerning accuracy could be the relevant thing in some other (less interesting) cases when we conclude that an observation statement is false. But, nevertheless, the major point is not one which merely concerns accuracy. Second, the auxiliary assumption queried by Lorentz and Fitzgerald was not one that a person would ordinarily even be aware of, let alone think of questioning. This causes us to realise that there will be many, perhaps an infinite number, of auxiliary assumptions underlying any seemingly incorrigible observation statement. Third, the point that there are always such auxiliary assumptions is not merely an abstract one, of no practical relevance, voiced by academic philosophers, which we believe we can safely ignore in the so-called real world. Rather, the events we have described above really did take place in the 19th century, bringing about a fundamental change in our view of the way things are. (Although we shall not discuss it here, the idea that moving objects contract in length, along the direction of movement, played a large part in the later formulation of Einstein's theory of relativity – a theory which has fundamentally transformed the way we envisage the world.)

MUST WE CONCLUDE THAT NO OBSERVATION STATEMENT IS INCORRIGIBLE?

There have been various attempts to avoid having to conclude that observation statements are not incorrigible. It is easy to appreciate why such attempts would be made, for surely we would wish to preserve the Standard View if we can, in that it provides us with a criterion for choosing between theories that everyone would accept, given that we are trying to find out what the world is like. Thus, we cannot show some theory to be true, but we can reject a theory that has been shown to be false, and thereby at least reduce the possible number of structures that the world could have. By contrast, if the Standard View is incorrect such that observation statements are not incorrigible, then the use of falsification as a criterion is no longer possible; for we can no longer say for sure that any theory that seems to have been shown to be false by experiment is actually false – it could be that some auxiliary assumption is false instead. And if we cannot use falsification as a criterion for choosing between theories, what criterion or criteria are we going to use? The nationality of the person who proposed the theory?! The answer is not at all obvious.

At this point the reader may have realised that the real significance of denying that observation statements are not incorrigible pertains to its implications concerning the criterion or criteria that we should use for deciding between theories. So given that we would like to hold fast to the Standard View if we can, in order to retain the criterion of falsification, let's consider two possible ways in which we might think we could save it.

One attempt to avoid the conclusion that observation statements are not incorrigible depends on the fact that experimental tests of a theory often involve the use of measuring instruments. For, as illustrated in the Michelson and Morley experiment, auxiliary assumptions tend to be made about the use of measuring instruments. Even the simple case of measurement of distance by a metre stick or time by a clock is measurement by an instrument, and it was an auxiliary assumption concerning the measurement of length by a metre stick that Lorentz and Fitzgerald queried. So, perhaps if we could devise experiments that do not use measuring instruments, we could avoid the problem. In order to consider this suggestion in more depth, it will, as you should come to appreciate, be helpful if we first explore in greater detail the

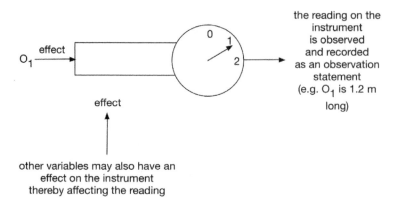

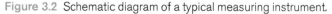

Figure 3.2 Schematic diagram of a typical measuring instrument.

characteristics of measuring instruments. We can then address the question of whether we could dispense with such instruments.

Suppose, as illustrated in Figure 3.2, we are using an instrument to measure the value (magnitude) of some variable which is an attribute of an object O_1 – say its weight, height, voltage, colour, or whatever. The measurement will be made by a determination of the effect the variable has upon the instrument. Note, however, that the effect will depend both upon the value of the variable and the properties of the instrument. For example, if the properties (attributes) of the instrument remain constant under all measuring conditions, then the different readings will reflect only changes in O_1 – just as it should do, given that it is a property of O_1 that we wish to measure. However, if the properties of the instrument vary as a result of the effect of other variables, then, to some extent, the reading will reflect those variations (see Figure 3.2). For example, if the instrument changes according to whether or not it is in motion, then the reading on its dial may differ from one occasion to another as a result of this change, and have nothing to do with variations in O_1. Thus, the readings may not invariably reflect only the magnitude of the relevant attribute of O_1, and we may draw the wrong conclusion as to its value. In Figure 3.2, we have assumed an instrument with a traditional dial to illustrate this point. However, the same point applies, whatever the instrument, an example of which we have already seen in the case of a metre stick where moving may affect its length and hence the measurement made. Or, to give another simple example, consider a glass thermometer containing mercury, such that an increasing temperature causes the mercury to expand, thereby causing it to rise within the tube. If the glass itself were to expand when placed within the medium (e.g. hot water), the temperature of which was being measured, then the mercury would not reach the point that would correctly reflect the temperature of the water.

Figure 3.2 enables us to appreciate the essential characteristic a measuring instrument must have in order that it can be used to measure correctly the magnitude of some attribute of an object (O_1). This is that the instrument does not vary as a result of any other variations in the environment – for if it did, then the reading on the instrument would reflect these variations in addition to the relevant property of O_1; and if we were unaware of this, we would interpret a reading as being solely reflective of that attribute of O_1.

There is a further important implication of what we have said here. Since the attribute of O_1 is measured only by means of its effect on an instrument, it is measured indirectly. It is this indirectness which accounts for the possibility of error, in that other variables may also contribute to the effect.

Given all that has been said above, you might accept that sometimes observation statements are not incorrigible – but only, you say, in cases where measurement is made using an instrument. That is, you say, "well, of course interpretation is involved when using an instrument because the so-called observation statement depends for its truth on an auxiliary assumption about the instrument" (i.e. that there are no other variables affecting its reading). And then you might say that when no instruments are used, there is no reason to suppose that a statement could not be interpretation-free. Is it possible to have such a case? Well, what about when we look at an object with the naked eye? It seems that we then see the object directly – there appears to be nothing between the object, as it is out there in the world, and our awareness of it. It seems that this apparently direct apprehension can be contrasted with the indirect apprehension that is mediated by an instrument and so avoids the problem that an incorrect reading may be given. Let's consider this suggestion further.

Suppose you look at a swan with the unaided eye, and on the basis of what you see, you write down the observation statement "This swan is white". It seems that this statement is interpretation-free. It seems that it is a statement whose truth does not depend upon other assumptions about the world. However, to show that the statement is actually not free from interpretation, all we have to do is suppose, for example, that the feathers of the swan emit a chemical which is transmitted through the atmosphere, such that the chemical affects our eyes, resulting in changes that cause us to experience white. So we must accept the possibility that the swan is actually blue. As shown in Figure 3.3, the situation is analogous to the one in which we use an

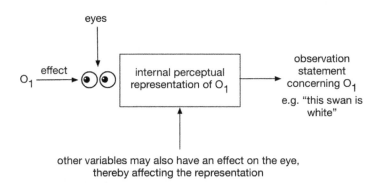

Figure 3.3 Schematic diagram of the eye as a measuring instrument.

instrument, in that the eye also is functionally an instrument: the impression we have of seeing the swan directly is misleading. There is no direct apprehension of the object – one's awareness is a result not only of the presence of the object, but also of the mediating eye – a result that comes about indirectly and could in part be determined by the effect of other variables.

Now, for clarity (nothing new will be said), let's work through Figure 3.3, depicting measurement by the eye, noting its essential similarity with Figure 3.2, in which it was more obvious that an instrument was used.

We have the observation statement "The colour of O_1 is white". But the supposed knowledge of the colour of O_1, as expressed by the observation statement, has come about by means of measurement by the eye. And if the properties of the eye vary, say according to the effect of some chemical which happens to be emitted by the swan's feathers (or, say, the velocity of the earth), then the percept may vary as a result of differences other than differences in the colour of O_1.

Now consider another means by which we might think we could retain the Standard View. Consider the following two possibilities. One would involve using a second instrument to measure properties of the first instrument to see how it works, and hence determine whether it does indeed measure what it is supposed to measure. The other would be by using a variety of different kinds of instruments (e.g. electrical rather than mechanical) to measure what we want to measure (e.g. some attribute of O_1). However, as should be obvious, in each case it could then be argued that just as one of our auxiliary assumptions about the properties of the first instrument may have been incorrect (allowing us to save the theory), so it can be argued that the same obtains in the case of any other instrument, for example, one that is used to measure some attribute of the first instrument. Hence, we cannot save the Standard View by using a variety of different instruments.

To illustrate further, let's work through a simple example to show what could occur when two people, Smith and Jones, believe different theories to be true: the theory held by Smith implies that all swans are white, whereas that held by Jones implies that all swans are blue. Each person observes the colour of the swan on the village pool and writes down "The swan is white". Thus, Smith believes that Jones's theory has been shown to be false. However, Jones then claims that the feathers of the swan emit a chemical that affects the eye, causing it to register the information that the swan is white, when actually it is blue. And, no matter how many other instruments are then used, say a spectrometer to detect colour or an instrument to detect the presence of the dye, Jones can maintain his or her position by claiming that these instruments are subject to effects that cause them to give incorrect readings, and insist on holding fast to his or her claim that the feathers emit a chemical that affects the eye. And the standoff between the theorists need not stop there. New possibilities of testing are opened up, which might make us think that the issue must eventually be open to resolution. So, for example, if the perception of whiteness that is experienced with the naked eye does indeed occur as a result of chemicals being emitted by the feathers, this implies the additional observation that the chemical should be found in the eyes. However, even if an instrument designed to detect chemicals in the eye fails to find evidence for the dye, Jones can claim that this instrument also is subject to effects that cause it to give an incorrect reading (i.e. 'no dye' when dye is actually present). And Jones can take a similar position every time there is some new apparent falsification of what he or she is claiming. Hence, no matter how many tests are carried out, it can never be shown that Jones's belief that the swan is blue is false.

CONCLUSION

The Alternative View seems to be correct from a logical point of view. There are no incorrigible (interpretation-free) statements one can make. Even statements that refer to observations, the so-called facts, are subject to revision. Quine (1951, p. 37) famously expressed this by saying "Our statements about the external world face the tribunal of sense experience not individually but only as a corporate body" (i.e. only collectively). What Quine meant by this is that we cannot take any statement (e.g. an observation statement or indeed any statement that expresses any one of our beliefs about the world) in isolation and know it to be true. Rather, all we can know, following the recording of some observation statement, is that either there is no contradiction between the various beliefs we hold, or that there is a contradiction. And in the latter case, there is no way in which one can say which particular belief or beliefs are false.

IMPLICATIONS FOR WHAT ONE IS FREE TO BELIEVE ABOUT THE WORLD

Upon first reading, the Alternative View may seem to imply that it gives us license to believe whatever we want about the world. However, this implication is incorrect. Nothing in what has been said implies that the claims made in science cannot be tested. Like the Standard View, the Alternative View asserts that all statements made in science must be open to test (albeit only collectively). For example, Michelson and Morley may have written down "Our theory predicts that the light will take X seconds to travel from one point to another" and, upon observation, written "The time taken was Y seconds". Thus, the statement from the theory and the observation statement are in conflict. Therefore, at least one statement concerning their beliefs about the world must have been false. So one cannot believe whatever one wants about the world.

What has actually been demonstrated is that the Standard View cannot be maintained. That is, it cannot be held that observation statements are incorrigible, and hence that any contradiction implies that it must be some statement within the theory that is false. Rather, it could be the observation statement that is false. As we shall now see, this conclusion does, neverthe-less, have profound implications.

CRITERIA USED TO DECIDE BETWEEN THEORIES

As we have already noted, if the Standard View were correct, it would be easy to decide which of two theories to adopt. We would just find some deduction from the facts that should obtain for one of the theories and not the other. Then we could make an observation to determine whether the fact obtains or not. We could then rule out the theory that is inconsistent with the fact, declaring it to be false, and retain the other as perhaps being true. However, according to the Alternative View, we can never say that there is some statement of fact which rules out one theory and permits another. That statement could itself be false, and hence there is no logical criterion for rejecting the one theory as compared with the other.

It seems, therefore, that we must keep both theories still under con-sideration. Yet, the fact is that in the history of science, some theories have been discarded in favour of others. Given this, we can ask what criteria scientists have actually used for deciding between theories (now that an unequivocal falsification of any theory has been shown not to be possible). And most importantly, we can then ask whether the use of these criteria can be justified (unlike, say, the preference for a decision made on the basis of a theorist's nationality). We consider these issues in Chapter 5.

Before then, in Chapter 4, we shall examine some more historical cases, additional to the Michelson and Morley experiment, which show in practice how scientists have responded when confronted with a contradic-tion between some observation statement and a theory. The examination of these cases will be used to further reinforce and illustrate the argument made above: that any test of a theory is actually a test of the entire body of one's beliefs about the world, thereby permitting one to save the belief that the theory is true by rejecting one or more of one's other beliefs.

1   Describe the significance of the Michelson and Morley (1887) experiment with respect to the interpretation of readings given by measuring instruments. What conclusions may be drawn concerning the possible falsification of theories? Discuss whether the acquisition of data by observation without the use of instruments might enable one to escape these conclusions.

2   Two scientists meet to discuss 'where we are at' in some particular domain of science. They think they might disagree concerning theory, and so adopt the strategy of first agreeing on the facts, before turning to theory to explain those facts. State where the error lies in this approach and explain its significance.

3   Discuss the significance of the fact that any scientific theory includes auxiliary assumptions in addition to the stated principles that are usually taken to characterise the theory.

4   "Our statements about the external world face the tribunal of sense experience not individually but only as a corporate body" (Quine, 1951, p. 37). Explain what this statement means and, using examples in illustration, discuss its relevance to the history of science.

5   It has been argued that observation statements are not incorrigible. State the argument and consider whether the problems can be solved by making observations using only the naked eye, without the use of measuring instruments.

6   Compare the Standard and Alternative Views of scientific explanation, and discuss their differences in relation to the criteria for accepting or rejecting a scientific theory.

Test your understanding of Chapter 3

CHAPTER 4

Some historical examples of responses to a contradiction between a theory and some apparent fact

We have argued that the Alternative View of science is correct: one can never test a single statement in isolation; rather, a test is always a test of the corpus of statements which comprise one's entire set of beliefs about the world – including the so-called facts (see Hempel, 1966, Chapter 7, pp. 88–90; Hesse, 1974, Chapter 1; Quine, 1951).

The significance of the Alternative View is that when there is a contradiction within the entire set of one's beliefs, it is always possible to retain any one belief by changing one or more of the others within the set. In the history of science, this implication has been important insofar as it means that, no matter what the evidence might seem to suggest, a scientist is never required to give up their belief that a particular theory is true. Instead, the scientist can retain the theory and change one or more of the other beliefs they have about the world. The reader may care to recall here, as the classic illustrative case, the Michelson and Morley experiment, and the response to it by Lorentz and Fitzgerald.

In this chapter, we will describe some historical examples (in addition to the Michelson and Morley case) which illustrate the point made above. Our aim in doing so is that we wish to reinforce what we have said above largely in abstract argument only. It will be helpful to keep in mind the scheme shown in Table 4.1, which shows how a scientist's entire set of beliefs/statements about the world can be categorised.

Note that the two categories of beliefs (stated principles and auxiliary assumptions) include all the beliefs that a person has about the world. Thus, the auxiliary assumptions include not only assumptions pertaining to the laws governing measuring instruments (as discussed previously), but also all other assumptions. Moreover, the person who has these beliefs is likely to be unaware of many of them until there is some reason for them to be articulated. For example, many of the readers of these sentences have the belief that they have no long-lost twin brother living in Australia, but probably they will not have been aware of having this belief until now. Consonant with this characterisation, auxiliary assumptions are sometimes called background assumptions (see Gillies, 1993, pp. 98–117).

Note also that the belief categorisation is not based on any fundamental distinction between principles and assumptions. It merely reflects the distinction between those beliefs that are being explicitly put forward as an

Table 4.1 Total set of beliefs/statements about the world.

Stated principles	Auxiliary assumptions	Observation statements
Laws and/or a theory	Often implicit and not articulated	
e.g. All swans are white	e.g. Swans do not emit chemicals that affect the eye	e.g. This swan is white

explanation (a set of laws or theory) of observed phenomena, and all other beliefs not presently under active consideration (auxiliary assumptions). As the reader may already appreciate, the distinction is, however, highly significant with respect to the fate of proposed explanations.

Let us now examine some historical cases of how contradictions between theory and observations have been resolved. In doing this, we could consider examples of three types:

1 Cases in which the theory has been abandoned in its entirety.
2 Cases in which the theory has been modified.
3 Cases in which some auxiliary assumption has been changed, thereby permitting the theory to be maintained in its entirety.

We shall consider only cases of the third sort, since these are the most interesting. They are the most interesting because they illustrate what has been argued previously: that it is possible *rationally* to maintain a belief in the truth of one's theory by changing some other belief or beliefs (one or more of the auxiliary assumptions).

EXAMPLE 1

The historical case of the Michelson and Morley experiment is the classic example. It will be recalled that Lorentz and Fitzgerald showed that a belief in the truth of the ether theory could be maintained by changing the previous auxiliary assumption that a measuring rod does not alter in length with changes in its velocity. Thus, they denied the truth of the observation statement "This length is x metres". In terms of the abstract scheme shown in Table 4.1, we can summarise the implication of what they did as follows: an auxiliary assumption was changed, thereby implying that the observation statement was false, thereby permitting the theory to be retained.

EXAMPLE 2

Newton's laws failed to predict accurately the correct orbit of Uranus around the Sun (see Hempel, 1966). Newton's laws predicted that the orbit was, say, x, whereas the observation statement reported it as being, say, y. So advocates of Newton's laws formulated the hypothesis that the deviation of y from x was the result of the attraction of Uranus, by gravitation, to an unknown planet in the vicinity of Uranus (see Feynman, 1967, pp. 23–24). Thus, they denied the previously implicit auxiliary assumption that no other planet lay in the vicinity of Uranus. The denial of this assumption permitted Newton's laws to be retained. Such a 'manoeuvre' might seem to be grasping at straws, but the change led to the prediction that a new planet should be seen at a particular location; and, upon observation of the location in which it was predicted to be, it was indeed seen (and the new planet was named Neptune). Of course, someone might question this latter observation, but as yet no one has.

Note that in terms of the abstract scheme described in Table 4.1, what was done in our second example is a little different from that done in the Michelson and Morley case. An auxiliary assumption has again been changed. However, this time the change has rendered the observation statement compatible with the theory, rather than denying its truth. You, the reader, might say that this case differs from that which best characterises the consequences of the Alternative View (the Michelson and Morley experiment), since the theory has been saved by a means other than rejecting the observation statement as false. We would agree with this. However, we have included it, and others of the same kind below, because we think it important to make the new point that once it is realised that one's overall world view includes auxiliary assumptions, thereby rendering the Standard View of explanation incorrect, the way is open to realising that there is more than one way in which changing an auxiliary assumption may save a theory. Changing an auxiliary assumption might imply that the observation statement is false (e.g., Michelson and Morley) or, alternatively, it might render the observation statement compatible with the theory, as in the case of the assumption pertaining to the presence of a planet in the vicinity of Uranus. Either way, the theory is saved. In the remaining examples below, we shall see that in each case, a theory was saved by changing an auxiliary assumption, resulting in either one of these outcomes.

EXAMPLE 3

Consider Darwin's (1859) theory of evolution, which asserts that the off-spring of any organism tends to differ from its parent in small random ways. If these differences are advantageous to survival, the offspring are likely to survive, and, in turn, may breed, yielding further offspring with further changes. In this way, an ancestral organism (e.g. a one-celled animal) could eventually give rise to a very different organism (e.g. a man).

Now, it is an essential part of this theory that advantageous changes 'accumulate' very slowly. This is so because such changes are only a small subset of all the changes that occur, and each individual change is very small in its effect. Therefore, the theory implies that the earth must have been formed billions of years ago. But, in Darwin's time, almost everyone believed that the earth was only a few thousand years old. Of course, Darwin had to deny that this was so (in order to retain his theory), but others were not prepared to deny it. For example, in 1868, Kelvin (see Dalrymple, 1994) put forward an argument against the earth being very old. In common with other members of the scientific community, Kelvin believed that the earth was formed from a molten mass of material, and that this mass had gradually cooled over time. And, using established laws of physics, he calculated that if the earth were very old, even its core should now have cooled. Yet the measured temperature showed that it was still hot (an observation statement). Kelvin therefore argued that the earth was, relatively speaking, quite young, and hence was led to reject Darwin's theory. As should be clear, Kelvin's rejection of Darwin's theory was not irrational. (It is also of some interest that Kelvin put forward an account of the origin of life alternative to Darwin's account. He suggested that primitive one-celled life forms reached earth by means of meteorites from other planets. Since no early evolution of such things on earth was required, this was, of course, consistent with the earth being much younger than Darwin had to suppose.)

However, an auxiliary assumption common to all scientists at that time was that there was no source of heat in the earth additional to that originally in the molten ball. Almost certainly this assumption was held without any conscious realisation of holding it and never made explicit (as far as we know, no person voiced it). Nevertheless, a Darwinian could have voiced it and denied its truth, assuming instead that there was some additional heat source. Thus, he or she could have argued that the earth, even though old, would still be relatively hot, and so could have readily maintained their belief in evolution. Now, had this occurred, it would perhaps have seemed that the Darwinian was grasping at straws. Imagine the derisive reaction of an audience if the supposition of an unknown additional heat source had been put forward at some lecture in an attempt to counter Kelvin's argument! It would have seemed tantamount to grasping at straws, for there was no independent reason to suppose that there was such an unknown heat source. However, in the 20th century, the element uranium was discovered. Uranium emits heat spontaneously – heat that does not originate from the original molten mass. And it is heat from uranium in the earth that accounts for the greater temperature of the core that Kelvin predicted from Darwin's theory. Hence, a typical (rational) scientist now happily accepts Darwin's theory of evolution, whereas previously they might have thought it must be false.

Note that, as in Example 2, the rejection of the auxiliary assumption (that the earth contained no heat source other than that arising from the earth's original molten core) rendered the observation statement (concerning the present measured temperature of the earth) compatible with the otherwise questionable theory.

Now consider a more recent debate about the theory of evolution. The carbon dating of fossils shows that, consistent with the theory of evolution, early life forms are much older than the few thousand years that creationists suppose. Nevertheless, creationists could question this evidence by questioning the correctness of the instrument readings that measure age by carbon dating. That is, they could challenge some relevant auxiliary assumption, pertaining to carbon dating, with the result that the readings on the instruments (observation statements) could then be deduced to be incorrect. They could do this by using exactly the same logic as Lorentz and FitzGerald when they questioned the then current belief about measuring rods in the Michelson and Morley experiment. And would their proposal be any the less plausible than the suggestion, made previously by the Darwinians, that there is an additional source of heat that could enable one to save the theory of evolution?! Similarly, creationists could, by one means or another, query the correctness of the measures taken of the heat emitted by uranium. That is, they could again change an auxiliary assumption with the result that the observation statements pertaining to these measures would be deduced to be false. And what they suggest could be true! Just as 'we' have now rejected Kelvin's auxiliary assumption that no heat was generated within the earth other than that present at the planet's birth, in order to save Darwin's theory, so others, in order to reject that theory, might reject the assumption that our measures of heat emission, and the measures of dating by carbon, are correct. So, are the creationists irrational? Well, in our experience they can sometimes do a very good job of 'explaining away' all the observations we take to be evidence of a much older earth.

Of course, one might reasonably expect the creationists to make some suggestion as to why the instruments used in carbon dating do not actually measure age, at least under the relevant circumstances. And when they have formed a hypothesis that states why this is so, others might test it. (Note, in passing, that as we are considering only suggestions that could be included within science, any suggestion made must be open to test – we would disallow any argument based only on what it states in the Bible.) And suppose we do test their hypothesis and suppose that the results of that test suggest that it also is false. Then the creationists could question the instrument readings or some further assumption we had made in the test of that hypothesis. And they could be right – it could be that that is the way the world actually is! And so, logically, it could go on and on, with one side retaining its belief that primitive life existed a long time ago and the earth is very old, and the other retaining its belief that neither of these is the case.

EXAMPLE 4

In the 15th century, it was generally held that, as proposed by the Greek philosopher Ptolemy, the earth is stationary with the sun and planets revolving around it. However, contrary to the prevailing view, Copernicus proposed that, contrary to intuition, the earth rotates around the sun. Copernicus's claim encountered difficulties because of various objections, based on assumptions then held concerning the size of the universe and the laws

Viewer stands at some location on earth at all times (e.g. T_1, T_2)

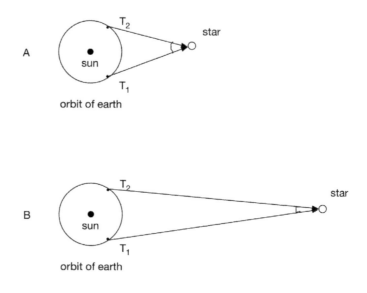

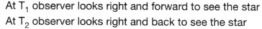

At T_1 observer looks right and forward to see the star
At T_2 observer looks right and back to see the star

Figure 4.1 Illustration of stellar parallax.

that govern motion. For example, it was asked (see Butterfield, 1957, Chapter 4; Hempel, 1966, pp. 23–24) why the position of a star did not appear to change direction during the supposed annual rotation of the earth round the sun, as would be predicted. We can explain this more fully by reference to Figure 4.1. Consider first, part A of the figure. The large circle depicts the supposed path of the earth around the sun (according to Copernicus). Suppose a person is located at a constant position on the earth. They look toward the star at time T_1 and note that it is to their right and a little forward of their own position. Then, later, at time T_2, they look at the star again. As shown in the figure, the star should be seen again to their right, but back a little. The angle between the two lines shown on the diagram is a measure of the difference between the two apparent locations of the star and is known as the angle of stellar parallax.

Now, when this experiment was carried out, no stellar parallax was found – the apparent position of the star seemed not to change. Such a result would, of course, be expected if the earth were stationary. Thus, this observation seemed to show that the earth does not move round the sun.

So what was the auxiliary hypothesis that was later claimed to be false? Well, it was assumed that the stars were much closer to the earth than they 'actually' are (see part B in the diagram). Hence, a large detectable change was predicted. But since the stars are actually (so we now believe) very distant from the earth, more than 700 times further away than was thought in Galileo's time, the degree of parallax is very small, requiring very sophisticated instruments to measure it. Note that this is another case when a change in an auxiliary assumption rendered the theory and observation statement compatible.

In this example, as in the case of Darwin, it is currently believed that Copernicus was right, and the auxiliary assumption then commonly held is false. It could have been the other way round (i.e. the auxiliary assumption is true and Copernicus was wrong). And, of course, there was no rational way of knowing at the time. And, in principle, we could again change our view, for it is conceivable that someone will argue that we currently make assumptions, perhaps without even realising it, which make it incorrectly appear that Copernicus was right. In other words, it is possible that our belief concerning the distance to the stars may change yet again.

SUMMARY: THE STATE OF AFFAIRS AT ANY ONE HISTORICAL TIME

The philosopher Lakatos (1978) examined the history of science to see what has been the fate of various theories. He pointed out that, contrary to what one might expect according to the Standard View, there is often no sudden permanent demise of some particular theory, rejected as false by virtue of some crucial experiment which yields findings contrary to the theory. Hence, there is no stepwise successive elimination of theories which have been shown to be false. Rather, a theory may fall from favour when the evidence seems to show it is false, but then some later development leads to its resuscitation, such that what previously seemed to falsify it is no longer considered to do so. Hence, sometimes a theory which was once thought to be false has later been thought to be true, just as in perhaps the more usual case, a theory which was thought to be true may later be thought to be false. Overall, at any one time there may be any number of competing theories, each intermittently rising and falling in favour. This is, of course, exactly what would be expected given the Alternative View, our analysis, and the examples given above.

Nevertheless, you, the reader, might be both sceptical and puzzled. Perhaps you can find nothing wrong with what we have said, but also you might point out that over some long period of historical time, some theories actually do fall by the wayside and seem never to recover. For example, you might now be asking yourself why it is that most present scientists so confidently believe that phlogiston theory (discussed earlier in our analysis of the Standard View) is false. And, actually, Lakatos also notes such long-term trends – some theories seem gradually to fade away, perhaps experiencing a number of rises and falls in favour as they do so. Thus, the question now arises as to whether some long-term trend of a decline of some theory is merely prejudice or fashion? If not, then presumably there must be some criterion or criteria by which theories are, in the long run, rejected, and then the question arises as to whether these criteria can or cannot be justified. And now you are puzzled as to what these criteria might be, and whether they can be justified, recognising that the criterion cannot be whether the theory has been shown to be false. Well, you would be right to be puzzled. In the next chapter, we shall address the puzzle.

Test your understanding of Chapter 4

1   Describe some historical cases in which what scientists now think to be true was, with good reason, thought by some to be false. Explain how this could be so, and consider what general conclusion or conclusions may be drawn.

2   According to Quine (1951, p. 37), "Our statements about the external world face the tribunal of sense experience not individually but only as a corporate body." Explain what Quine means by this assertion. Illustrate your answer by reference to some historical cases in which claims made in science about the world have been tested.

3   The history of science suggests that, even when confronted with an apparent refutation of a theory, an advocate of that theory could rationally maintain that the theory should not be discarded. Describe and discuss some historical case to illustrate this. What general lessons do you think can be drawn with respect to what theory a non-committed scientist should adopt?

CHAPTER 5

The criteria used for choosing between competing theories

We have seen that more than one theory can always be put forward to explain a set of data. For example, S-R theory can account for the ability of rats to learn the shortest route to food in a maze, but so can Tolman's (1948) theory, which postulates an internal cognitive map, and one that is strikingly different from S-R theory (see Chapter 2). In such cases, it has traditionally been thought (the Standard View) that we can decide between two theories by identifying some difference in prediction between the two, testing by making some new observation, and discarding the theory which is inconsistent with the supposed newly discovered fact (as expressed in an observation statement). Hence we can retain the theory which, in relation to this test, survives unscathed, and discard the other. (One should, of course, appreciate that the theory that is retained might fail some later test.) Thus, a falsification of one of the theories is the criterion used to select between competing theories.

But now contrary to the Standard View, we have seen that this procedure does not guarantee that the theory which failed to predict the result correctly is at fault. Instead, the fault may lie with some auxiliary assumption, such that if that assumption were to be rejected, then either the observation statement would no longer be thought to be true or the observation statement would be seen to be consistent with the stated theory. In either case, the basis for discarding the one theory in favour of the other would no longer obtain. Moreover, there is no way in which it can be determined which assumption, or assumptions, in one's entire set of beliefs (theory plus auxiliary assumptions) is at fault. Hence we can never know whether it is the theory or some auxiliary assumption which is false. As Quine (1951) says, any one assumption can be retained by making suitable adjustments to others.

In summary, falsification cannot be used as a criterion for deciding between theories. What criteria, therefore, are to be used to select between theories, and can such criteria be justified? We shall consider two possibilities.

AXIOMATIC BELIEFS

Historically, many scientists have preferred one explanation to another because the preferred explanation has properties which are consistent with their fundamental beliefs about how things must be. That is, they say that it is axiomatic (a starting principle which, for them, cannot be questioned) that things must be a particular way. Thus, the strength of their commitment to the relevant properties is very much greater than a commitment to the typical auxiliary assumption – which does not have this 'must be the case' status and which, although perhaps unwillingly, they would be ready to change. Some examples of selection according to whether a theory conforms to a theorist's axiomatic beliefs, taken in historical order, are as follows.

EXAMPLE 1

As we have seen, the Aristotelians believed that a body will move only when being pulled or pushed by some force (e.g. a cart being pulled by a horse). However, this raised a problem as to how to explain the movements of the planets, the sun, and the stars around the supposedly fixed earth. The problem arises because these movements occur apparently without any 'push' or 'pull' being exerted upon the moving bodies. At first, some thought the movements must be the result of angels pushing the bodies. But others, noting that the movement of some of the bodies is more or less circular, claimed that circular motion by heavenly bodies is natural in that it requires no explanation (i.e. does not require any explanation by reference to something else – for example, push or pull). Only non-circular motion requires explanation. (We, the authors of this book, do not know why they claimed that circular motion was 'natural'. Perhaps it had something to do with the idea that a circle is a perfect form – although it is not obvious to us why a circle should be thought to be more perfect than, say, a square. However, be that as it may, planetary movements still posed a problem since it was observed that they are not exactly circular (and sometimes deviated greatly from circularity). So how were the deviations from circular motion to be explained? An explanation was given by superimposing circular motions upon circular motions (see Figure 5.1). This enabled the advocates of the explanation to account for all the observations that had been made up to that time by reference only to supposedly natural circular motions. As may be appreciated by looking at Figure 5.1, an analogy would be to suppose that a wheel travels round a circular track and that an object travels in a circle around a point at the end of one of the spokes of the wheel. The resultant movement of the object through space would not itself be circular, but could be decomposed into circular movements (see Butterfield, 1957, Chapter 2). In summary, then, given the axiomatic belief that circular motion is natural, a 'reduction' of non-circular motion to circular motion was taken to provide a preferred (not merely satisfactory) explanation of the observed motion.

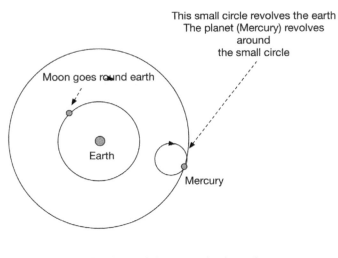

Figure 5.1 Movement of the planets as explained by circular motion.

EXAMPLE 2

Newton explained the circular movement of the planets around the sun by a combination of two of his three laws. As we have seen, one of these laws states that "All bodies remain in a state of rest or uniform (straight line) motion unless acted upon by some external force." Hence, once in motion, a planet will continue to move in a straight line (see Figure 5.2). The other law he used was the law of gravitational attraction. As we have again seen previously, this states that any two bodies (e.g. the sun and a planet) attract each other over a distance. This law explains why the planet circles round the sun, rather than flying off at a tangent (i.e. continuing in a straight line). As shown in Figure 5.2, the two laws used in combination yield the deduction that the planet will move in an approximately circular motion round the sun.

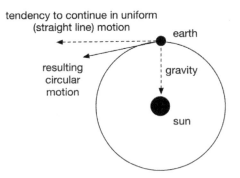

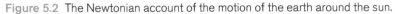

Figure 5.2 The Newtonian account of the motion of the earth around the sun.

Now, how did others react to Newton's explanation? Let's consider their reaction to the law of gravitation – the law relevant to what we want to say. One thing others did not deny was that the law was expressed precisely in mathematical form and that it enabled one to deduce (predict) the path taken by the earth around the sun exactly. It could also be used to deduce the occurrence of many other phenomena. Hence, in these respects the law was entirely satisfactory. Nevertheless, some did reject it as an explanation of the various phenomena. Descartes, and others, thought it *impossible* that one body could be attracted to some other body, when only space lay between them. That is, he rejected the possibility of a force being able to act at a distance and argued instead that there must be some local interaction between the bodies if one is to affect the other.

One possible way in which local forces could produce the attraction was devised by Feynman (1967, pp. 37–39). Feynman devised his account in a context different from the one being discussed here, but it is worth considering his account in the present context to illustrate what is meant by 'local force'. Suppose that the whole of space is 'occupied' by many small particles, each moving in a random direction, and too small to be seen by the naked eye. Suppose also, for the moment, that the universe contains only one large spherical mass. Then particles would be striking the mass more or less equally from all sides since their impact would be more or less constant over the entire surface of the sphere; and hence the body would remain (almost) motionless. But now suppose that there were two such masses as shown in Figure 5.3. In such a case, although particles would be striking each mass directly on a path that would run through their two centres, there would be no particles travelling such a path within the space separating the masses. Hence the masses will move toward each other as a result of the pressure of the particles on the far sides of the two masses – and the effect will be greater the closer the bodies are to each other – just as Newton's law predicts. So Descartes would have accepted such a mechanism as a possible explanation.

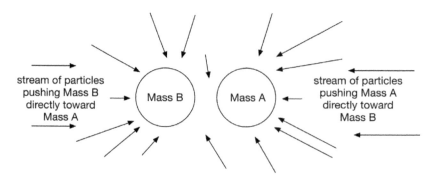

Figure 5.3 Depiction of local forces as a cause of gravitational attraction (based on Feynman, 1967, p. 38).

Unfortunately, however, as Feynman points out, for reasons we shall not describe here, the proposal also implies the occurrence of additional effects that are not obtained (see Feynman, 1967, p. 38, for details). Hence, the proposal must be rejected.

EXAMPLE 3

Prior to the 20th century, a fundamental belief held by scientists was that nature is deterministic: that is, if some particular event A causes event B, then any other occurrence of an identical event A will also cause event B. For example, if a billiard ball A of a certain weight, and speed, strikes another stationary billiard ball B of a certain weight, such that B moves forward a particular distance, then any replication of the initial conditions will be followed by B moving forward that same distance. Then, early in the 20th century, the theory called quantum mechanics was put forward to explain a variety of effects found in experiments carried out to examine the atomic composition of objects. Quantum mechanics differs fundamentally from all previous theories in that it assumes that nature is inherently non-deterministic. For example, consider the emission of electrons from any radioactive material. According to the theory, an emission will occur following a certain interval since the last emission with a certain probability. Hence, given a constant antecedent state of a slab of uranium, an electron is sometimes emitted and sometimes not following that interval. Or, put another way, if there were two *identical* (not merely similar) slabs of uranium, one slab might emit an electron at time T_1, whereas the other may not. Thus, rather than there being a law of the sort "Whenever X occurs then Y follows", the law states "Whenever X occurs then Y follows with a probability of 0.6" (say).

The lack of determinism is inherent in the theory. To make clear what this means, we can contrast it with what is assumed in psychology. In psychology, just as in quantum mechanics, we use statistics because we are uncertain of what will occur. However, in psychology, statistics are used only in order to take into account the effects of variables of which we are ignorant. That is, we assume that variations in behaviour occur 'merely' as a result of unknown variations in the state which is antecedent to that behaviour. This can be illustrated by the fact that if we had identical twins, with exactly the same environmental history, and now under exactly the same conditions, we would predict they would behave in exactly the same way. Moreover, if our understanding of human behaviour were complete, we could predict unequivocally what this behaviour would be. (Hence, there would be no need for statistics.) By contrast, in quantum mechanics, we don't use statistical analysis to take account merely of our ignorance about unknown variables. Rather, according to quantum mechanics, there are no unknown (hidden) variables: nature itself operates probabilistically. Nature is inherently non-deterministic.

Now, the theory of quantum mechanics has been extremely successful. Nobody has ever carried out an experiment which has produced a result which contradicts the theory. And the theory explains all the basic properties of matter (not just the emission of electrons from uranium). Yet Einstein rejected the theory. Why? He rejected it because, as he is reputed to have said, "God does not play dice" (see Rae, 1994, p. 48). That is, he accepted as axiomatic the assumption that identical events in nature are always followed by identical effects. (It is of some interest also to note that Bohr, a theorist who played a large part in the formulation of quantum mechanics, is believed by many physicists to have replied, "Don't tell God what to do!" – again, see Rae, 1994, p. 48.) As a final aside for readers who would like to learn more about quantum mechanics, we would recommend starting with Feynman's (1967, Chapter 6) account of the famous two-slit experiment or a more general account given by Rae (1994).

In recent times, it is often said that any preference based on axiomatic beliefs is arbitrary and cannot be defended. Looking back on historical examples, this seems obvious. And so we like to think that we have no such beliefs. Thus, Russell (1913) says that the only requirement for a theory to be acceptable is that it enables deductions to be made – that is, if X then Y (including when Y is probabilistic). Not even cause and effect are required. But, perhaps as something of a digression, we might ask whether we are now as free from axiomatic beliefs as we think we are. Consider the following.

Suppose that, as shown in Table 5.1, over successive moments of time T_1–T_6, the entire state of the universe at any one time (i.e. everything that exists at that time) can be described as: A (everything that exists at T_1), then Y (everything that exists at T_2), then B, then C, then Y, then D. For convenience of exposition, note also that the sequence of six states can be divided into two triads A, Y, B and C, Y, D. Thus, what we have in this (changing) universe is a dependency of the contents of the third member of a triad B or D on the contents of the first member of that triad A or C with the intermediary, second member (Y), being common to the two triads.

Suppose also that all subsequent sequences of events conform to this pattern; that is: AYBCYDAYBCYDAYBCYD . . . and so on for all future time.

In other words, we have what looks like a cause leaping over time to produce its effect: state A is always followed by B and state C is always followed by D, such that the intervening state (Y), being common to the two triads, could play no part in accounting for why B rather than D (or D rather than B) occurs as the third member on any one occasion. Such a phenomenon is analogous to Newton's action at a distance. Ordinarily, we assume that a cause cannot operate over temporal gaps just as Descartes and others assumed that a force could not operate over spatial gaps. We now accept

Table 5.1 Possible leap of effect over time.

T1	T2	T3		T4	T5	T6
A	Y	B	then	C	Y	D

the latter, but may find it hard to accept the possibility of the former. So perhaps we have not entirely discarded using axiomatic beliefs as a criterion of theory preference.

Some readers may find it difficult to understand this example. However, we do not think this is because it is poorly explained! Rather, we suggest that, at least in part, it is because the assumption that action over time must be local (unlike the example given above) is so deeply entrenched in our belief system that we find it difficult to think in any other way. Perhaps this was true also for the Aristotelians and their belief about circular motion, or Descartes in his belief that action at a distance is impossible.

CAN SELECTION ACCORDING TO ONE'S AXIOMATIC BELIEFS BE JUSTIFIED?

Suppose the Standard View were correct. It would then, almost certainly, be agreed universally that the criterion used to reject one theory as compared with another should be falsification. The use of this criterion would be justified in that it advances our knowledge of how the world actually is. Or, more precisely, it would tell us how the world is not, and hence would limit the possibilities of how it must be. By contrast, it may not be possible to justify other criteria for distinguishing between theories (as required by the Alternative View). Suppose, to take an example similar to one given earlier in this chapter, that someone were to use as a criterion, the selection of a theory that had been formulated by a Scottish rather than an English person (or vice versa). Surely we would agree that this criterion could not be justified – in no relevant sense does it pick out the better of the two theories. Hence, we just would not accept this as a criterion.

So, can selection according to one's axiomatic beliefs be justified? We do not think so. Surely(?) these beliefs just happen to be basic beliefs that a particular culture or group has at a particular time in history, and hence the theory selected is no more likely to be superior, in any acceptable way, than one which would be selected according to the basic beliefs of some other culture.

POWER, SCOPE, SIMPLICITY

We now turn to consider a second possible criterion for selecting between theories: that of selecting the theory which has the most power, the greatest scope of explanation, or is the most simple. According to this criterion, a good theory is one which explains a variety of apparently disparate facts by means of only a few principles. For example, Newton's three laws explain the seemingly very different movements of the planets, projectiles, pendulums, the ocean tides, and billiard balls. Before Newton, it had not even been realised that events in the heavens and events on earth are governed by common principles. Newton was a great scientist. To many, it seems self-evident that when choosing between theories, one should choose the simplest – that is, choose the one which has the most power: the one for which the number of explanatory principles is smallest as compared with the number of different (disparate) kinds of events explained by those principles.

In psychology, S-R theory is a good example of a simple and powerful theory in that its advocates claim that it accounts for all behaviour, other than that which is innate, solely in terms of the few principles of association (contiguity, frequency, and reinforcement) and stimulus generalisation. Or consider connectionist versus symbolic accounts of cognition: connectionist accounts make fewer assumptions than symbolic accounts. For example, they show that complex language processing can arise from simple connectionist accounts. In one well known and much discussed case, the pattern of development of regular and irregular past tenses of verbs (e.g. kissed as compared with ran) has been shown to emerge from without any additional assumptions, whereas symbolic accounts require an additional learning of rules (see Elman, 1998; Pinker & Ullman, 2002).

HISTORICAL EVIDENCE FAVOURING SIMPLE THEORIES

As previously noted, Lakatos (1978) has examined the history of science (see also Bechtel, 1988, pp. 50–63, pp. 68–70). And as we have seen, he accepts the Alternative View of science and its implication that in the history of science, there cannot have been a successive elimination of theories which have been shown to be unequivocally false. In this context, he looked at the historical record to see how one theory has, in fact, eventually come to replace another. As we have seen, he notes that theories do not die suddenly as a result of one supposedly crucial experiment (as the Standard View implies they should); rather, they seem to gradually fade away. Furthermore, we can now note that he claimed that the theories that seem to fade away are ones which, perhaps gradually, have become overburdened by complexity. Clearly, this is exactly what would be expected if scientists take simplicity as their criterion for selecting between theories.

Note that on first reading the paragraph above, one might conclude that the original fundamental characterisation of science as the study of that which is open to test by observation is no longer appropriate. One might think this is because we are now focusing on a criterion (simplicity) for a selection between theories which may seem to have nothing to do with test by observation. But it would be wrong to draw this conclusion. When Lakatos (1978) said that theories become overburdened by complexity, he was typically referring to a process whereby the increased complexity has been brought about by some test which reveals a contradiction between an observation statement and the entire set of beliefs that the scientist has had, until then, about the world (i.e. beliefs expressed in the theory and beliefs expressed in auxiliary assumptions). For it is the modification of these beliefs, carried out in order to resolve a contradiction, that often brings about the increase in complexity. And of course this process may be repeated any number of times such that eventually, any allegiance to the theory may just fade away as the complexity becomes correspondingly even greater. The following expands this idea further.

An extreme case of the tendency of scientists to reject theories of little power (i.e. ones that lack simplicity) is exhibited in their typical disparagement of *ad hoc hypotheses*. An ad hoc hypothesis is a hypothesis put forward to save a theory when the hypothesis serves *only* to bring about a compatibility between the theory and some particular refuting observation. The classic example given in the textbooks (e.g. Hempel, 1966, pp. 28–29) concerns an early theory as to the contents of space. The basic principle of the theory was that nature abhors a vacuum. This explains, for example, the finding that when air is exhausted from a container by a suction pump, it tends to rush into the container through any opening. However, Périer showed that the disposition for air to rush in was less on top of a mountain than at its base – consistent with the present view of scientists that it is air pressure which accounts for the effect (see Hempel for details). Thus, the basic principle was refuted (or perhaps we should say was shown to be inadequate). So the advocates of the "nature abhors a vacuum" principle proposed an additional principle, namely that "nature abhors a vacuum less on top of a mountain than at its base." This was an ad hoc hypothesis in that although it saved the theory by accounting for the one anomalous case, it played no part in explaining any other finding. As Hempel points out, such a hypothesis is generally considered not to be a good saving hypothesis because it yields no further deductions, and therefore increases the complexity of the 'theory'.

Note that the objection is not that the ad hoc hypothesis is necessarily false; rather, it is that it decreases the power of the theory, for it constitutes a new added assumption, with only a single new observation being explained.

Another good example of the additional complexity of a theory that results from the proliferation of additional assumptions can be seen in the various claims of the creationists, put forward in order to retain their belief that the earth is only a few thousand years old. Each additional assumption they put forward to save the theory is ad hoc – it serves to account for just one awkward finding, for example, the readings given by carbon dating, which they wish to explain as reflecting something other than the age of the earth. Thus, in the extreme case, one ends up with a very large number of explanatory 'principles', each being used to account for just one fact.

It may be noted in passing that ad hoc assumptions are to be distinguished from post hoc assumptions. Ad hoc assumptions are assumptions that are introduced merely to account for one anomalous fact and play no part in the explanation of other facts. By contrast, to say that an assumption is post hoc is merely to say it was put forward to explain a fact after that fact became known. Such an assumption may or may not also be ad hoc. It is ad hoc if it explains only the one fact, thereby increasing the complexity of the theory. So, for example, "Nature abhors a vacuum less on top of a mountain than at its base" is both post hoc and ad hoc. By contrast, the assumption is not ad hoc if it is seen to explain not only the single fact which suggested it but also a number of other facts, which are now, for the first time, brought under the umbrella of the theory – thereby maintaining its simplicity. As far as we can see, it is of no great importance whether an assumption is post hoc or not – it is merely an accident of timing. Admittedly, the fact was not predicted, but nevertheless it can be deduced from the new assumption. And surely it does not matter, with reference to the structure of the explanation, whether the fact is deduced before or after it is actually discovered.

Lakatos (1978) also claims that theories tend to flourish when they correctly predict striking new phenomena. It seems unlikely that such flourishing can be explained by reference to simplicity. However, it does have a plausible explanation which we now include just to show that it is not in conflict with simplicity. The explanation is as follows. Insofar as a prediction is striking, it is one that is not made by other extant theories. (If it were, then surely it would not be striking.) Therefore, such a prediction not only supports the theory under consideration, but also shows that there is something wrong with all alternative theories presently held. Hence, at least until the others are amended in some way, the theory that made the prediction is the only acceptable one.

CAN A CRITERION OF SIMPLICITY BE JUSTIFIED?

Given that the historical record shows that scientists have usually preferred the simpler of two different theories, we shall now continue to focus on this criterion and ask whether such a preference can be *justified*. It may *seem* self-evident that one should choose the simplest explanation – but is it? Surely it has to have some justification. Let's see if it can indeed be justified. We consider three possible justifications.

Truth

The first possible justification we shall consider is one pertaining to the possible truth of a theory. Arguments have been made in the literature to support the claim that a simple theory is more likely to be true than a more complex theory. However, counter-claims have been advanced to refute these arguments. (For a variety of views, see Grunbaum, 2007; Sober, 2002; Swinburne, 2010; Zellner, 2002.) Some of the arguments involve sophisticated reasoning, concerning probability and statistical concepts that we shall not discuss here. So, we could say that the issue is unresolved. However, with some hesitation (for we believe that attempting to answer this question is akin to walking through a minefield), we offer the following analysis.

The issue of whether a simple theory is more likely to be true than a more complex theory concerns the case when two different accounts, one simple and one complex, have been put forward to account for a particular set of observations (X). We shall restrict ourselves to the case where the accounts postulate unobservable entities (i.e. theories in the strict sense, e.g. kinetic theory, as opposed say to laws, e.g. Newton). Consider the population of all possible universes. Two subpopulations are of particular interest in addressing the issue. They are as follows:

1   Each member of one subpopulation is a simple universe in which a small number of unobservable entities produce observations X. Moreover, in addition it has the property that a deduction of these observations could be made from a more complex (false) account.
2   By contrast, a complex universe is one in which a large number of unobservable entities produce observations X, and, in addition, has the property that a deduction of these observations could be made from a simpler (false) account.

Now, if it is assumed that these two possible populations are of equal size, then the particular universe we live in is no more likely to be a simple one than a complex one. In other words, in order to show that it is more likely that the universe we live in is a simple one, we must question the presumption of equal likelihood of the two kinds of universe. That is, one has to postulate some constraint on universes, the consequences of which would be to favour simplicity. It is not clear what this constraint could be or on what grounds it could be supposed. And, for those who might contemplate a divine origin of the universe, we suggest that we should not assume that, in his choice of what sort of universe to create, God created a simple universe rather than a complex one. As Bohr said to Einstein in another context (discussed earlier in this chapter), "Don't tell God what to do." Our conclusion is therefore that a scientist's preference for a simple theory cannot be justified on the grounds that a simple theory is more likely to be true than a complex one.

Prediction

We now consider a second possible justification for the selection of simple theories. It could be argued that what we want primarily in science is prediction – and we want prediction for its utilitarian value – to enable us to control physical events and thereby live a better material life. Moreover, it can be argued that, in general, a simpler theory can generate more predictions than a more complex one, thereby justifying a preference for simple theories.

However, we shall now argue that, for scientists, prediction does not provide a justification for preferring simple theories simply because many scientists do not greatly value either prediction per se, or prediction for its utilitarian value. We shall attempt to show this by describing two illustrative cases. The first case is a hypothetical one, but one which we believe is particularly clear in illustrating the relevant points.

A soothsayer is a person who claims to be able to predict the future. Such persons are typically found, for example, at fairgrounds or village fetes. Now, let us suppose, for the sake of argument, that a soothsayer was able to predict correctly the effect of any change in the world, for example, the result of any experiment a psychologist might want to carry out. In addition, suppose that when we ask the soothsayer how they manage to do this, they can only say "I have no idea! All I know is that if you ask me to make a prediction concerning something or other, an answer just comes into my head and I respond with that answer." Now, given what is essentially a potentially infinite list of correct predictions that the soothsayer can make available to us, would scientists still be interested in formulating theories to explain the predicted events, even though we have, from the soothsayer, the knowledge to engineer any conceivable practical manipulation we desire? Well, some scientists might not, but others, we suggest, would. Although these latter scientists might value prediction for practical reasons, as non-scientists also do, they would not be content with prediction only. They would say that prediction alone is not sufficient for what they want. For, in addition to prediction, they want to know why or how the predicted events occur. In this context, it can be noted that in the 16th century, the movements of the tides could be predicted, with great accuracy, from timetables constructed by having observed the tides on each day over a period of many years. And these tables greatly assisted navigation on the seas. Yet there were scientists who were interested to know why the tides varied as they did.

As something of an aside, it may be appropriate here to remind the reader that prediction in science is important, but in a sense only in that it is valued as a tool. As discussed extensively in the earlier chapters of this book, prediction is required in order to test theories (including relevant auxiliary assumptions). Their tool-like nature can readily be seen by considering further a world which includes our hypothetical soothsayer. It seems to us that in that world, scientists would formulate their theories just as they do now, but instead of carrying out experiments to test those ideas, they would simply ask the soothsayer what the result of a particular test would be. In such a world, nothing much would change, in doing science, other than that the scientists would save themselves a lot of work!

The second case which illustrates that many scientists do not greatly value either prediction per se, or prediction for its utilitarian value, concerns Darwin's theory of evolution. Darwin's theory is one theory in science that is simple, but makes very few predictions, and yet scientists consider it to be one of the most impressive theories ever articulated. Darwin's book *On the Origin of Species* (1859), which led to the general acceptance of this theory among scientists, consists largely of observational findings which are explained by the theory and are exactly of the sort that the theory might be expected to predict; yet it cannot do so because it is insufficiently specific in any particular case. In order to make this clear, let us remind ourselves of what the theory says. Darwin's theory states that during mating, the genetic material that determines the constitution of the offspring has a random disposition to mutate (change). Most mutations reduce the ability of the offspring to cope with their environment – coping activities such as finding food and escaping from predators. Therefore, these animals are likely to die before mating. Hence these mutations are not passed on to subsequent generations. But some mutations, a very few, happen to be advantageous to survival in the particular environment inhabited by the animal. Hence the animal is more likely to survive and mate than other members of the same species that lack the mutation. Therefore, these mutations are likely to be passed on to its offspring. In this way, over a number of generations, animals with a common ancestor may, in different environments, come to diverge (vary) greatly in their characteristics, each being specialised according to its own particular environment.

Now, what other account could be simpler than this account? (Huxley, a contemporary of Darwin, is said to have exclaimed "Why didn't I think of that?") But note that the theory predicts almost none, if any, of the particular variations/differences we can presently observe between species (i.e. the data). Rather, each variation 'merely' conforms to the pattern prescribed by the theory. This idea can be illustrated as follows. Suppose we consider a single-celled animal existing, say, one billion years ago. In the subsequent billion years, there may have been any number of particular mutations in the generations of offspring, all effectively random. And each of these may or may not have been advantageous within the particular environment in which the animal then lived. Now, given this, it is clear that we cannot predict/ deduce the present existence of many specific animals or perhaps even a single specific animal – animals such as human beings, chimpanzees, spiders, and sharks. But, nevertheless, the presence of many small variations between members of some species at the present time and in the fossil record shows how both the small differences and the larger differences (each resulting from an accumulation of smaller differences) conform to the general pattern we would expect. Thus, the theory provides a general template to which any account of a particular observed variation seems to conform, thereby providing both an explanation of how species came about and rendering uninteresting many seemingly intractable questions that previously puzzled scientists and thinkers – questions such as: how did it come about that the bee and the flower are so admirably suited to facilitating the reproduction of the other?

Of course, one may still be interested in answering a particular question such as that pertaining to the bee and flower, or other questions concerning the particularities of the evolution of any one species, but this would now be just routine science. The theory has largely already done its stuff in explaining how the variety of animals and plants came about. One no longer lies awake at night desperately thinking "What on earth (so to speak) is going on here?" Specific predictions, with some notable exceptions (see below), had to wait until the discovery of genes, approximately a century following the acceptance of the theory. It seems to us that the theory of evolution provides a strong counter-example to the supposed justification of simplicity on the grounds of prediction. Darwin's theory is simple and yet makes few predictions.

Finally, in this section we should make clear the following point. We are not saying that either of the two cases we have considered shows that scientists must be motivated by a desire to understand why events take place; perhaps many scientists would be satisfied with utilitarian prediction alone. And we do not see how one could argue that having a motivation solely for prediction, for understanding, or for both, is the 'right' motivation – it is just a matter of what one wants to achieve by doing science. Nevertheless, the general conclusion we draw from both the Darwinian case discussed above and the case concerning the Soothsayer is that scientists are primarily concerned with understanding the world; and therefore we shall now, in turning to our third possible justification for preferring simple theories, explicitly make (or perhaps reinforce) this claim.

Explanatory content

We now consider the third of our possible three justifications for preferring simple theories rather than complex theories. One outcome of our preceding discussion is that we have come to appreciate that scientists typically (even if not always) want to know how/why events occur. Perhaps this realisation might be the key to providing a justification for choosing the simpler of two theories. We shall now consider this idea (see also Toulmin, 1961). As we have seen, Darwin's theory of evolution explains a very large variety of the different forms and behaviours of different species of animals and plants by means of only a few principles (random variation and selection of the fittest). So, to this extent, the theory is a simple theory. However, you, the reader, could point out that a complex theory might also explain the great variety of life forms we observe – so why should we prefer the former? The explanatory content would seem to be the same (i.e. number of events explained). One possibility, the one to be considered here, emerges from an appreciation that one can ask for an explanation not only of what we have observed, but also for an explanation of the explanatory principles themselves – for example, how do mutations come about – what's the mechanism? And, clearly, fewer of these questions will arise in the case of a simpler theory, merely because there will be fewer principles to which we can address the how/why question. Hence, overall, it can be argued that, even when two theories explain more or less the same number of observations, the simpler theory has greater explanatory power in that it leaves fewer unresolved questions to be asked at the level of the principles/theory which explains those observations. Thus, if, as argued above, explanation is what is typically desired, a preference for simple theories can be justified.

At this point the reader, whilst accepting what has been said above, might raise a point concerning testability. The preceding discussion might appear to suggest that Darwin's theory is not open to test, and therefore is not a scientific theory. But as we saw in Chapter 4, it is open to test. For example, insofar as advantageous mutations are rare, small, and cumulative, it can be predicted that measures of the age of the earth will show that it is very old. (The reader may recall that Kelvin rejected the theory on the grounds that he thought he had discovered that the earth was not as old as required by Darwin.) One can think of other tests also. For example, the theory predicts that in layers of rock which are conducive to the preservation of fossils, no evidence of any sudden change from any one species to another will be found; for instance, there should be no sudden change from primitive ape to man, but there should be evidence for the occurrence of many small intermediate changes, as can indeed be observed.

Now, for clarity, let's illustrate the entire argument by reference to our old friend, kinetic theory and the behaviour of gases. The illustration is somewhat unrealistic, but is, we believe, illuminating. First, we may note that kinetic theory is a simple theory in that it postulates just unobservable small particles, their random movement, and changes in their velocity. The theory proposes that heating the gas increases the speed at which the particles move. Hence, it explains why the heating of any gas in an enclosed chamber increases the pressure on the walls of the chamber – any one particle hits the walls more frequently and with greater force than it did before heating. And insofar as gases differ from each other, they differ according to how much their speed increases and therefore the pressure they exert. So what questions are now raised concerning these explanatory principles? Here are several we can think of. Why do the particles move? Why does their speed increase when they are heated? Why do the particles of some gases exhibit a greater increase in speed than others? How many particles are typically present in a given volume of space, and does their number vary? Perhaps there are more questions, but anyway, the total number is not large.

Now consider, for contrast, an illustrative alternative theory to explain the increase of pressure that occurs with an increase in temperature – one of extreme complexity, just to see what such a theory would look like. (Do not object that the alternative we shall describe is highly implausible – that does not matter; we are using the example only for illustration.) Let us suppose that instead of kinetic theory, which describes any gas as consisting of very small particles, we had a different set of theoretical statements describing a different structure for each type of gas (e.g. one for oxygen, one for carbon dioxide, and so on). Thus, we would have an explanation for the entire range of gases that is more complex than kinetic theory. The reader may prefer to think of this as a set of different explanations, one for each type of gas (it makes no difference to the argument). Now let's go further in reducing simplicity. Suppose that for each individual instance of each type of gas, someone were to propose that the behaviour of the gas was the result of some structure (mechanism) peculiar to that particular instance. For example, one account would specify the structure of the oxygen contained in a particular canister in a particular hospital in Chicago in 1968, whereas another different structure would be proposed for a canister of oxygen in a

London hospital in 2010. Then all we would have would be a collection of explanatory mechanisms, with each being related to the others in no way whatsoever except insofar as each accounts, in its own way, for some particular observed increase in pressure with temperature. In such a case, we would have the same number of explanatory mechanisms as observations. Hence, insofar as we would like to explain the explanatory 'principles', the number to be explained would be as great as the number of observations they explain! In other words, the number of how and why questions remaining is no less than it was before the explanations were put forward. Thus, our conclusion, as suggested earlier, is that the more complex a theory, the less is its explanatory power.

It is worth noting one additional point about adopting explanatory power as a criterion for selection of one theory over another. In Chapter 2 it was noted that Poincaré showed that it is logically possible that two different theories might make exactly the same predictions, and therefore, in such an, albeit rare, case, a criterion of differentially rejecting just one of them on the basis of some observation (the Standard View) could not be used. The point worth making now is that choosing a theory based on the criterion of explanatory power might permit a decision to be made between the two. One would reject the theory with the least explanatory power (except in the extremely unlikely case that the two are equal in this regard). We, the authors, do not believe that this could be presented as a major argument in favour of adopting the criterion concerning explanatory power, but it is worth noting.

Newton's laws provide another good illustration. The three laws enable one to predict exactly the direction and speed of movement of billiard ball B when struck by ball A, moving towards B with *any* known velocity (speed) from *any* known direction. And, by contrast, if we were to formulate a different qualitative account for each different event to be explained, as we did with the gases, we would have an enormous number of explanatory principles, which themselves are not explained.

In the preceding discussion of the justification of simplicity on the grounds that simple theories provide a greater degree of understanding of how the world might be, we have as yet used theories only from the traditional sciences to illustrate the arguments being made. What about psychology? In Chapter 2, we examined in detail the contrast between representational theories of learning (Tolman's cognitive map) and S-R theory. And we showed how a simple basic S-R theory could be falsified. However, S-R theory is actually one of many versions of learning by association, with the idea common to all being that if any two events of a particular kind occur in close temporal proximity, they will become associated (connected). A version of this general idea was advanced by Hume in the 18th century, with sensations being the associated events. Hume claimed that seeing one billiard ball striking another, followed immediately by seeing the second ball moving away from the first ball, led to an association between the two such that on any subsequent occasion of seeing one ball striking another, the observer would have an image (expectancy) of seeing the second ball moving away from the first ball. And in another version of associationism, Hebb (1949) postulated that it was the firing of neurons that became associated. Hebb proposed that if an external event caused some neuron to fire, and then shortly thereafter a different external event caused another neuron to fire, then a connection would tend to be formed between the two neurons such that any subsequent firing of the first neuron caused the firing of the second neuron (again yielding something similar to an expectancy). Thus, according to Hebb, a process of association played a large part in the development of connections in the nervous system with any increasing experience of the world. Moreover, since the demise of basic S-R theory, other versions of associationism under the heading 'connectionism' have been proposed. Why are these theories so popular (to put it crudely)? One plausible answer is that they are simple: each theory postulates just the one simple principle, and yet seems open to the possibility that it can account for the entire variety of behaviours which arise as a result of a person or animal learning about its environment, including social behaviour and mental illness.

Some readers might object to the claim that scientists typically prefer the simplest explanation available by pointing out that many theories, for example those that describe the structure of the human body and its operations, seem to be concerned primarily with 'seeing how things work,' in standard mechanical or chemical terms, without bothering too much about simplicity. Nevertheless, the simplicity principle is applicable here also insofar as it is possible to reduce the proposed explanations to statements of basic physics and chemistry. If the explanations did not tie in with what has been learned in physics and chemistry, it is conceivable that we would not accept them.

Finally, it should be recognised that there is something of a paradox in suggesting that although scientists seek maximum explanatory power in selecting the simpler of two theories, they have no grounds for assuming that the simpler theory is true. But it is only a paradox (not a contradiction): if, as seems plausible, the simpler theory is no less likely to be true than the complex theory, then, as described above, it would make sense to select the simpler theory on the grounds that it provides the greater explanatory power.

In this context, we suggest that readers who have not seen the film *2001: A Space Odyssey*, directed by Stanley Kubrick, should treat themselves to an instructive viewing. In the first few scenes of the film, which depict the 'Dawn of Man', a giant obelisk, constructed from some smooth, seemingly unearthly material, is shown standing in an area of open ground within the jungle. And then from all sides of the jungle emerge a number of ape-like humans. They warily approach the structure, and tentatively, fearfully, jab it with their outstretched fingers, testing and probing its structure; and slowly they begin to learn about it (and become less fearful in the process). Surely, we suggest, this is what the latter part of this chapter has been about, namely our innate curiosity. It is this which drives science, with the preferred theories being those that, in most greatly increasing our understanding, most greatly satisfy that curiosity.

SUMMARY

We shall now summarise what we have said concerning theory preferences, given the truth of the Alternative View. It follows from the Alternative View that we cannot have a supposed unequivocal refutation and rejection of any theory on the basis of experiments that contradict that theory. Therefore, criteria other than falsification have to be used in deciding between theories. Two such criteria (axiomatic beliefs and simplicity) have been used in the history of science. So, the issue arises as to whether either of these can be justified. It has been argued in this chapter that simpler theories provide a greater understanding of what is observed than complex theories, and on these grounds, the use of simplicity as a criterion for selecting one theory over another can be justified.

One lesson that might be learned by practicing scientists, regardless of whether they agree with what we have said about the criteria used for selecting between theories, is that they should be ready to accept the continued investigation of any explicitly stated principles which seem to be on the downward slide (as measured by apparent refutation). Such theories could exhibit a resurgence following a change in some auxiliary hypothesis.

Test your understanding of Chapter 5

1 In the history of science, what criteria have been used to evaluate theories? Can any of them be justified?

2 Philosophers of science and scientists have often advocated the use of particular criteria to determine their preference for one theory over another. Describe some of these and state which one or ones you would use, giving the reason or reasons for your choice.

3 Describe and evaluate the contributions of Popper and Lakatos to the Philosophy of Science. (See Chapter 2 for discussion of Popper's contribution and the present Chapter 5 for discussion of Lakatos's contribution.)

4 Using examples in illustration, describe the relevance of post hoc and ad hoc hypotheses in the modification of theories when these are confronted by anomalous data. Explain why ad hoc hypotheses are generally considered to be unsatisfactory, and discuss whether or not this can be justified.

5 Write an essay on simplicity as a criterion for preferring one theory over another.

6 "Science is not a matter of forecasting (prediction) alone, for we also wish to discover explanatory connections between the happenings we predict" (Toulmin, 1961, p. 16). Discuss this claim, and consider the relevance, if any, of the disposition of scientists to favour simple accounts of their observations.

Summary of Part 1

The characteristics of scientific explanation

1   Structure of scientific explanation. Scientific explanations include statements that describe observations, laws, and theories. We discuss two views. The Standard View asserts that, although the truth of any statement that specifies a law or theory is open to doubt, observation statements describe facts that are not open to doubt. By contrast, the Alternative View is that all statements within science are open to doubt. Thus, according to the Alternative View, even statements that supposedly describe facts may be questioned. Hence, science cannot be built upon a bedrock of unequivocally established facts. The implications of this were discussed.

2   Explanations must be subject to test (i.e. open to falsification). It was shown that, as implied by the Alternative View, any test is always a test of one's set of beliefs taken as a whole, rather than of a single identifiable assumption within a particular theory.

3   Treatment of recognised anomalies. We considered the various ways in which explanations can be amended to take account of apparently refuting data. The case in which a theory may be saved by changing background (auxiliary) assumptions is of particular interest. Examples from various sciences, including psychology, were discussed.

4   Choosing between competing theories. What criteria do scientists employ in choosing between competing theories? Can any of them be justified? We argued that a criterion of simplicity can be justified on the grounds of explanatory power and an ability to make predictions.

PART 2

Understanding behaviour

In these six chapters, we examine different approaches to understanding behaviour and mental operations. In addition, we consider some of the personal and social consequences that may result either from an acceptance of the assumptions made in taking some particular approach, or the advances in knowledge that empirical research may bring.

CHAPTER 6

Typical approaches in psychology

Internal mechanisms

Scientists and non-scientists alike attempt to understand and explain the behaviour of human beings and other animals. In this chapter and the next, we shall discuss a variety of approaches taken by scientists in their attempt to understand such behaviour. In particular, we shall ask what counts as an adequate explanation of behaviour in psychology. Most psychologists assume that the behaviour of a person results solely as a result of physical operations, and we shall make that assumption ourselves in these two chapters. Other issues, such as the possibility of free will or some involvement of consciousness, will be discussed in later chapters, for they require extensive consideration in their own right.

Even within the limitations imposed by the assumption that behaviour is a result solely of physical processes, a number of distinctive approaches can be taken. Our aim will be to describe these different approaches and their differences, taking illustrative cases from work which shows the differences most clearly. We shall not attempt to bring the reader up to date with respect to the most recent experimental and theoretical work unless it serves this function.

THE PSYCHOLOGIST'S GOAL

Psychologists may seek any one of three distinct kinds of scientific explanation, each associated with a different goal. All three can be illustrated, in outline, by reference to Figure 6.1. Figure 6.1 depicts the connections between the environmental input to a person, the successive operations carried out upon that input within the person, and the consequent behaviour that follows. Each operation is carried out (implemented) by some physical mechanism, such as that involving the action of neurons or hormones. An assumption held by the vast majority of psychologists, which we shall accept in this chapter, is that the sequence from environmental input to behavioural output constitutes a continuous causal chain.

We can think of the whole person (or some other animal) as a black box, by which we mean that ordinarily the internal operations that link the environmental input to behaviour are hidden from view (for example, the skull conceals the internal operations carried out in the brain). The psychologist

Figure 6.1 Connections between environmental input, operations, and behavioural output.

may wish to understand any of three aspects of the entire system, according to their goal.

a) The goal of some is to discover the internal operations carried out which, within the black box, convert the environmental input to the behavioural output, without having any concern for their physical embodiment (the physical mechanisms which actually implement the operations). The following analogy may help to make this clear. Suppose we are interested in understanding the circulation of the blood around the body. Any of a variety of mechanisms could implement the operation, such as a muscular structure (the heart) or an electrical motor, the latter having been inserted when a diseased heart is replaced by an artificial device. However, one might take the view that all we are interested in is the operation of pumping, regardless of how that operation is physically implemented. Similarly, most psychologists have taken the approach of attempting to understand behaviour without reference to the physical hardware that implements the operations which yield that behaviour; and that is the approach we shall examine in this chapter.

b) Alternatively, the goal may be to discover both what the internal operations are and how they are embodied physically, for example, by the action of neurological or chemical changes. This approach could be taken either for its own sake or for its potential use in medicine – for example, when a serotonin deficiency is hypothesised to be the cause of depression. Some sorts of physiological psychology aim for this goal, in particular within the field known as cognitive neuroscience. The approach requires some understanding of the nuts and bolts of chemistry and physics, one which is beyond the scope of this book to discuss. Therefore, we shall not examine it.

c) A third alternative goal is to identify only the effects of possible environmental inputs to the person (or animal) upon their behavioural output, without any reference to the intervening operations which link the two. This attempt solely to gain knowledge of the laws that relate behaviour to the environment was advocated primarily by Skinner (1950), and has had many adherents since. These adherents are often referred to as Skinnerians. We shall discuss the Skinnerian approach in Chapter 7.

Since different psychologists adopt different goals, it may be that the ideas and experimental work thought valuable by one may not be thought valuable by another. However, it might also be that there will be some cross-fertilisation. For example, it is possible that a person who is interested in the physical implementation of operations carried out within the brain might make a discovery which, in suggesting that a particular operation is being carried out, may be of interest to the individual who is interested only in the specification of operations without reference to hardware. We shall not discuss these possibilities in detail, but we shall see that some discussion of them is almost inevitable in the course of exploring how the different goals may be best achieved.

For the remainder of this chapter, we shall discuss in detail the sort of account typically advanced by those who seek to achieve the first of the three goals described above.

INTERNAL OPERATIONS WITH NO REFERENCE TO EMBODIMENT

Figure 6.2 schematically depicts the operations carried out within the black box, with each operation being enclosed within a rectangle in order to make it clear that it is only the operation being carried out that is of interest, rather than the physical means by which it is carried out. We shall call each one of these rectangles a unit. Thus, by definition, a unit is a physical entity (the particular composition of which is of no interest) which carries out some operation. Consonant with what we have previously said, the physical nuts and bolts of a single unit may be located in more or less the same location in the brain or scattered throughout the brain, or with any distribution between these two extremes. But since we are not interested in the physical implementation of any operation, we represent the unit which carries out the operation by a neutral rectangle. Figure 6.2 depicts a greatly simplified version of a chain of units which brings about behaviour as a result of some environmental input. In practice, there may be more than one environmental input at the same time (e.g. visual and auditory); and regardless of the number of inputs, there may be all kinds of feedback loops and alternative pathways linking units within the black box. However, the number and complexity of these pathways makes no difference to the basic logical properties of explanations of this sort.

The essential characteristic of an explanation of this type is that each unit is specified in terms of two requirements. The first requirement is a

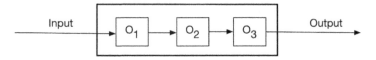

Figure 6.2 Schematic diagram of a complete chain (no breaks in the chain) of operations from environmental input to behavioural output. O_1, O_2, and O_3 refer to successive operations.

description of what the unit does: that is, the operation it carries out on its input, changing (transforming) it into some new form. For example, by analogy, in a radio set one unit may select the signal transmitted by a particular station from the multitude of signals present at input and another may amplify the selected signal. And similarly, in the input stages of visual processing in the human being, a unit may operate upon information coming from just one part of the overall visual field.

The second requirement of a unit is that its location within the sequence of units should be specified. (Try putting the loudspeaker in a radio set before the amplifier – it won't work.) The location of a unit within the sequence of units determines the input to that unit. For example, if unit A is linked to unit B such that A immediately precedes B, then its output is the input to B. Note that by location, we do not mean spatial location. Rather, as stated above, we mean the location of the unit within the sequence which results from all the units being linked to other units. By analogy, in the case of the radio set it is irrelevant that the amplifier is, say, to the left or right of the loudspeaker: what matters is its location within the chain of units, starting with the radio signal at input and ending with the loudspeaker at output.

GRANULARITY OF EXPLANATION

Before we go any further, we have to decide what level of granularity it is appropriate to employ in an explanation. That is, what size of operation do we wish to describe and use in our explanation? Do we seek to describe a finely grained, massive network of primitive operations, each of which, in the extreme case, may 'merely' pass its input signal on, as input, to other identical operations (in which case, as we shall see later, different behaviours would be explained solely by different patterns of connections among the units)? Or would we prefer to discover whether there are fewer operations, which, by virtue of each consisting of many simpler operations in different arrangements, carry out a 'larger' unique operation – such as the detection of faces (Gross, 1992) or the recognition of words? Insofar as one is interested only in such larger operations, without regard for their possible mapping onto more basic elements, we could say we are interested in understanding the relation between the environmental input and behaviour at a coarse-grained level. In order to show more clearly what it means to understand behaviour without reference to the physical embodiment of the internal operations, we shall, somewhat arbitrarily, first consider examples of explanation when taking a coarse-grained approach.

Coarse-grained analysis

Explanations of this type are typically the goal of cognitive psychology. Consider, for example, the following explanation of word recognition, based on Morton's (1969) influential logogen model. For simplicity, we shall consider only the recognition of words which are presented visually. The contents of the black box include a bank of information which uniquely specifies the ideal characteristics of all possible visually presented words (for example, 'DOG'). Recognition of a word is a product of all stored information relevant to what that word might be, plus the present visual input. We can consider how a word is recognised by reference to Figure 6.3 (which looks complicated but will be seen to make sense as we work through it). Let's begin with the store labelled general knowledge and meaning (see Figure 6.3). This store includes information about the meanings of words and the frequency with which any particular word has been previously presented. Its output serves as a more or less continuous input to all the members of the entire bank of possible words. We shall be concerned with just one of these (the one that specifies the characteristics of the word 'DOG') to illustrate the workings of the entire mechanism. The output from the store constitutes the input to Unit A. It is operated upon by Unit A, yielding an output that either lowers or raises a threshold in Unit C. This raising or lowering of the threshold makes it more or less likely that any future sensory input – for example, a degraded version of the word 'DOG' – will be classified by Unit C as an instance of

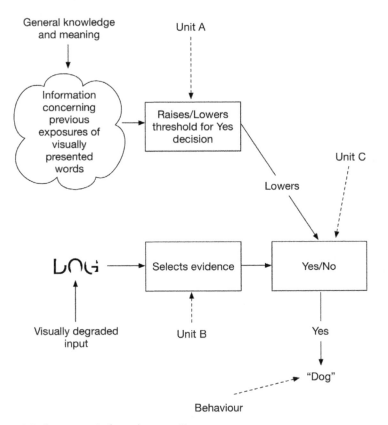

Figure 6.3 An account of word recognition.

that word. Figure 6.3 depicts a case in which it lowers that threshold. Unit B selects evidence from the current visual input (the degraded word 'DOG') that is consistent with the word being 'DOG' and then forwards it to Unit C. The operation carried out by Unit C determines whether or not the evidence is sufficient in magnitude to cross the threshold which obtains at that time. If the input crosses the threshold (as illustrated in the figure), then the sensory input is deemed to be the word 'DOG', resulting eventually in the behavioural utterance "dog".

A number of behavioural effects can be explained by the account. For example, as described above, it accounts for our ability to classify degraded words as instances of that word. It also accounts for the faster naming of a word (e.g. dog) when it has been preceded by the presentation of a word similar in meaning or association (e.g. cat). This effect is explained by the lowered threshold (gate) previously brought about by the input (cat) from the general knowledge system. In similar fashion, the theory also explains why a word which occurs frequently in the relevant language is recognised more quickly than a word which occurs with low frequency. It does this by supposing that previous presentations of the word have reduced its recognition threshold. Many other theories of particular cognitive abilities also postulate units of this coarse-grained sort, as a glance at any cognitive psychology text (e.g. Eysenck & Keane, 2015) will confirm.

The attentive reader may have noted that we have postulated just three distinct operations (A, B, and C) in the preceding account of word recognition, and to that extent it is coarse grained. But why not go the whole hog and, in order to illustrate the characteristics of coarse-grained accounts further, provide an account with the coarsest grain possible – just one operation? Let's try that. Suppose that the sensory information was said to be the input for a unit, the operation of which was "classification of the input as a particular word." And that would be it – one single operation and nothing else. Well, in that case we would make the wrong predictions. To illustrate this, note that we would have made no reference to the knowledge and memory store. And as a result, the degraded input shown in Figure 6.3 would presumably not be classified as any word – even though the experimental evidence shows that it would be classified as the word 'dog'. So our account would be falsified. Similarly, we could not account for the word-frequency effect. This realisation illustrates an important point, namely that not all behaviour can be accounted for at the greatest possible coarse-grained level of analysis (i.e. one unit). Moreover, in the case of some theories of other behaviour, the same deficiency may arise when explanation is attempted at the next level down, or the next – or whatever. We shall discuss this point again later.

Fine-grained analysis

Consider again the coarse-grained account of word recognition shown in Figure 6.3, and in particular that part of the account pertaining to the decision as to whether a current sensory input includes enough evidence to pass the threshold for it being a particular word. We have already concluded that this constitutes a more fine-grained analysis than one that refers to the single operation of recognising a word. But we can, should we wish, examine what happens at a different level. The sensory input and the ideal word may differ in any number of ways – for example, the curves of some particular line, the angle between two particular lines, and the length of each line. In an even more fine-grained analysis, the description of the relatively coarse-grained operation of comparing the present sensory input with the ideal word would be 'replaced' by a description of a much larger number of more finely grained operations, each focusing upon evidence concerning different aspects of that input – for example, the features concerning angle and lines described above. And, similarly, all other operations within the black box would be concerned with the analysis of fine detail.

So, given our basic explanation of what constitutes a fine-grained analysis as opposed to a coarse-grained analysis, let us now look at one general current approach that has been taken to formulate fine-grained analyses of the relation between environmental input and behaviour.

CONNECTIONISM

The preceding paragraphs of this chapter have been largely concerned with what might be called 'traditional' assumptions concerning the processing that occurs within the brain: primarily the assumption that at a coarse-grained level of analysis, there are chains of encapsulated units, each carrying out a single operation such as word recognition (see Figure 6.3). In more recent years, challenges to this assumption have been mounted. We now examine one of these, but not because the traditional approach has been widely rejected. Scientists are always trying to think of new ways of looking at things, even when the ones already established have not been shown to be wrong (and even though particular theories that exemplify a given approach may have been shown to be inadequate or incomplete). It is in this spirit that we now describe the approach known as connectionism, an approach that first became prominent in the latter part of the 20th century. Connectionism presupposes an analysis at a much finer grain of analysis than we have considered so far. Thus, a typical connectionist account of behaviour assumes that there are a very large number of very simple units, massively interconnected. The number of postulated units may be hundreds or thousands or more, limited only by the computing power required to test the account.

Unlike the coarse-grained approach, each unit typically carries out the same single operation as every other unit, with any one unit being activated by one or more preceding units and carrying out the operation of passing on that activation on to other units. Different behaviours result solely by virtue of the occurrence of different configurations of the units and the strengths of the connections between those units. Thus, the work is largely done by the many interconnections between identical simple units as contrasted with the coarse-grained approach, in which the work is accomplished by a variety of fewer units (each of which presumably consists of any number of differently arranged component parts, accounting for the possibility of a variety of units). Whether or not the component 'fine grain' operations that constitute each of the operations in the coarse-grain analysis of cognitive processes are the same as those postulated in connectionism is an open question.

One can think of connectionism as being the heir to S-R theory (see Chapter 2 for a detailed account of S-R theory). In both cases, the number of different types of unit assumed is greatly limited, and a typical effect of an environmental input requires the involvement of many such units, often yielding a sequence that connects a unique behavioural response to some unique environmental stimulus. There are, however, two notable differences between S-R theory and connectionism. First, S-R theorists favoured something very close to a tabula rasa at birth (a blank sheet: no connections between stimuli and possible responses are present at birth, with the initial emission of a response to any stimulus therefore being random). In a typical connectionist system, no such assumption is made, thereby permitting a greater range of possibilities. Second, in S-R theory all adaptive behaviour was assumed to be brought about by learning, with a connection being made between a stimulus and response solely as a result of the stimulus being followed in close temporal proximity by what would become the response – an assumption of temporal contiguity that is the essence of S-R theory (see Hull, 1943). See also Hebb (1949), who later postulated that the temporally contiguous firing of any pair of spatially proximal neurons caused them to become connected. By contrast, this assumption (restriction) also is not necessarily made in connectionism. Nonetheless, the typical connectionist network is able to learn, with one possible learning algorithm being error correction, whereby the values of the links are changed to reduce the difference between desired and actual outputs. Connectionism may also be compared with S-R theory in another respect. S-R theory includes a major role for stimulus generalisation, but the generalisation is the simple one of generalising from one point to another on a single qualitative continuum. For example, there may be a generalisation from a stimulus such as the wavelength of light corresponding to red to the occurrence of a stimulus of the nearby wavelength of orange, but not to the stimulus of a distant wavelength such as blue. By contrast, connectionist accounts can explain a degree of generalisation which is not based solely on the distinctions between points on a single qualitative dimension such as wavelength. For example, some researchers argue (although these claims are controversial) that they can explain how individuals learn to produce the past tense of verbs, after being presented with a sufficient number of examples in which the past tense is produced by adding -ed to the present tense of a verb (kissed, killed, pricked). Computer simulations have shown that some connectionist networks would be able to produce the past tense of verbs that it has not been taught – e.g. kicked (Harley, 2014). The extent to which this sort of model can generalise or form novel abstractions is still debated.

Some psychologists may consider connectionist theories to be more plausible than traditional cognitive theories, simply because they do not believe that there are coarse-grained units (such as those we discussed earlier, that supposedly account for word recognition). But apart from any such consideration, connectionist models have had successes: they can learn, and their ability to exhibit stimulus generalisation if faced with a novel or distorted input means that they do not immediately grind to a halt, but can generate a reasonable guess as an output. Moreover, some connectionist networks are robust in that damage to part of the system does not lead to its immediate collapse; and they frequently demonstrate emergent phenomena in that sometimes they exhibit adaptive behaviour that was not explicitly programmed into the simulation of explaining the effects for which they were designed. Connectionist models also have the advantages of being very explicit in how processing occurs, and what assumptions are needed to get them working. In having these characteristics, they address issues such as whether the occurrence of some particular novel behaviour is, as one might ordinarily suppose, innately determined (c.f. Chomsky, 1965). Connectionist models have been applied to a wide range of cognitive phenomena, such as speech production, word recognition, language development, dementia, and visual processing (e.g. Rumelhart, McClelland, & the PDP Research Group, 1986; see Quinlan, 1991).

However, a note of caution may be added. We noted earlier that a coarse-grained analysis may sometimes be inappropriate because it is too coarse to always make correct predictions/deductions. However, in the case of fine-grain analyses, a different problem may obtain. Although the computation of thousands of operations may inherently yield predictions, the analysis may not, in any sense that we find acceptable, be understandable. (See Chapter 5, and in particular some relevant discussion concerning the predictions made by a soothsayer.) In this context, it may be of some interest that a similar issue also sometimes arises elsewhere in science. Thus, with respect to quantum mechanics, Atkins (2004) remarked that it is best to forget about understanding and just calculate. Similarly, Feynman (winner of a Nobel Prize for physics) is often quoted as having said of quantum mechanics that if you think you understand it, you don't understand it. Perhaps the same might apply with respect to fine-grained accounts of behaviour in psychology! If so, the attempt to formulate such accounts might be acceptable to some readers of this book and not to others.

SOME ADDITIONAL IMPORTANT POINTS

The following points apply equally to coarse- and fine-grained analyses of behaviour:

1　A complete specification of all the units (operations) and their locations within the entire sequence of operations, from environmental input to behavioural output, would enable one to deduce what the behavioural output will be. In practice, as you may have already realised, a strict deduction of the behavioural output is never actually achieved because no theory yet formulated even begins to specify the entire sequence of units linking environmental input to behaviour. However, plausible assumptions may often be made which fill the gaps (the unknowns) in an entire sequence. For example, in the case of our own account of word recognition, assumptions are made about the units governing the recruitment and coordination of the muscles used in executing a behavioural response.

2   If the predicted output of the proposed sequence of operations fails to match the behaviour of the person or animal whose behaviour in that situation one is attempting to explain, then the theory is incorrect.

3   In having the two properties described above, the theory is similar to atomic or kinetic theory (see Chapter 2). That is, the theory, which postulates entities (operations) which typically are not in themselves observed, yields a prediction of some effect that can be observed, providing thereby a test of the adequacy of the theory.

4   Given an interest in explaining the behaviour of some person, the question arises as to how one goes about formulating a theory as to what the relevant operations are that account for the behaviour. Typically, the formulation of a theory proceeds by trying to think of a sequence of operations that would produce the relevant behaviour. Usually, this task is not an easy one because there are no known rules for formulating adequate theories, and therefore an exercise of one's creative imagination is required. The same applies, of course, with respect to explaining the behaviour of heated gases (kinetic theory), and many other effects in science.

5   As in the other sciences, it is always possible to formulate more than one theory to explain a particular relationship between environmental input and behavioural output. (As we saw in Chapter 2, for any theory, the data can be deduced from the theory, but the theory cannot be deduced from the data.) Hence, one cannot be confident that some particular sequence of operations which would explain some known behaviour is the correct sequence.

6   As stated earlier, explanations of the type we have described are sought generally by those whose major goal is to *understand* how behaviour comes about. It could, however, also be argued that such understanding, as well as satisfying human curiosity, is useful in that it may enable one to predict and control behaviour. For example, if we understood what operations were carried out by the brain in processing visual information to yield the perception of scenes, we could, perhaps, programme computers to do the same thing. Nevertheless, the prediction and control of behaviour is not usually the primary goal. (In this respect, the approach may be contrasted with that of Skinner – see Chapter 7.)

We have now provided a basic description of the approach taken by those psychologists who wish to discover what operations link environmental input to behaviour – without any interest in the specification of the hardware by which this is accomplished. Now, given a commitment to such a goal, let's address an important question that is seen to be an obvious one to ask once it is raised.

DIRECT INSPECTION OF INDIVIDUAL UNITS

As we have seen, psychologists typically attempt to figure out what operations transform the environmental input into behaviour by looking only at the effects of the former upon the latter, and then making inferences as to what the internal linking operations are. However, there are two very good reasons why it could be very helpful if they were able to look inside the black box.

One of these reasons is that looking inside the box would seem to be the obvious way of discovering what operations are carried out within it. A strong case can be made for attempting to examine the brain and other internal organs directly in order to achieve the kind of explanation presently under consideration. Even though we may not be interested in the physical embodiment of the operations as such, we might directly examine the brain as a means of identifying what operations it carries out. Rather than inferring the entire sequence of operations that collectively yield some behaviour, an attempt could be made to isolate each operating unit individually. Ideally, we could then identify what each unit does by measuring its input and output, with the difference between the two measures telling us what operation it carries out (see Figure 6.4).

Thus, direct inspection would enable us to avoid the psychologically difficult exercise of formulating the theories that are required in attempting to make inferences as to what operations are carried out from knowing only the relations between the environmental inputs and behaviour. It would seem that one could merely look inside the box and record what is present. Direct inspection might seem to be the obvious way of investigation on the practical grounds that it would most readily lead to the discovery of what the operations are.

The other reason why it would be desirable to look inside the black box is as follows. Suppose two different theories can account for all possible

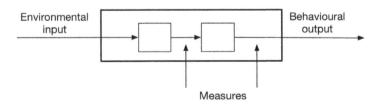

Figure 6.4 Measuring directly what an operation does.

environmental input/behavioural output relations. How then could we decide which theory to adopt? Presumably we would, at present, choose the simplest (see Chapter 5). However, if, instead, we were to look inside the black box to see which sequence is the one actually present, we could, on discovering that the postulated operations of the one theory (or perhaps even both) were absent, thereby falsify that theory. Hence, on these grounds also the question arises as to why psychologists traditionally have not looked in the box. Let us now address this question.

First, it is considered unethical to carry out experiments on individuals, and sometimes other animals, when there is a danger that it would cause damage or pain to the individual; and historically this would have been the case in research of the kind we have been discussing. However, as we shall shortly see, this problem has, to a degree, now been circumvented.

Second, we might find that the physical structure of the brain (its anatomy) is not ideal for discovery by direct inspection. In particular, it may not be obvious, certainly in the case of a coarse-grained description, what anatomical structure constitutes a unit and where its inputs and outputs physically lie. For comparison, consider an old-fashioned radio. It consists of spatially discrete 'objects' connected by wires. Each spatially discrete object carries out a single operation, for example, the amplification or selection of the signal from one station rather than another. Now suppose a Martian, knowing nothing of radio sets, wants to understand how the radio works by constructing a circuit diagram (that is, a diagram which does not include the details of the physical structure of the units) of all the internal operations. He or she opens up 'the box' and finds 'blobs' of matter (spatially discrete entities) connected by wires. It is then a fair bet that each blob constitutes a unit, thereby executing a single operation. Thus, it is easy to see what 'anatomical' structure implements a unit: it is any blob having wires entering and leaving it. So the Martian measures the input and output of each blob by taking measures at the points where the wires enter and leave. Hence, in this more or less simple fashion, which requires considerably less thinking than making inferences from the unopened black box (the radio set), the Martian discovers by direct inspection what operation is carried out in each case. And, by analogy with what the psychologist wishes to do, the Martian may then, without any reference or interest in the hardware that he or she has been examining, depicts the connections between the operations in the form of a circuit diagram. By contrast, it is doubtful whether the human brain, even under ideal circumstances of exposing its functional constitution, could be anywhere near as tractable as that of the radio.

However, since the end of the 20th century, techniques have been devised which provide some access to the internal structure of the black box in non-invasive ways that cause no damage. However, we are still far from being able to make direct measurement of inputs and outputs, and perhaps we shall never be able to make such measurements with the clarity that we would have when opening up a radio set. Nevertheless, the techniques we presently have for looking inside the box, although limited in what they can show us, are useful. We shall now consider these in more detail.

One means of gaining access to the inner state of the black box is that of functional magnetic resonance imagery (fMRI). In fMRI studies, there is typically an independent behavioural variable and a dependent behavioural variable. For example, the participant has to read aloud a word on a computer screen, and a measurement, taken in the form of a magnetic image, shows which parts of the brain are active during the process that links the participant seeing the word and speaking it aloud. Other techniques, such as magnetoencephalography (MEG), involve measuring small changes in the brain's magnetic activity while the participant carries out some task; MEG can pinpoint activity with much greater temporal resolution than fMRI. It is also possible to stimulate parts of the brain and observe how that changes behaviour; at present (2016), the best-known such technique is transcranial magnetic stimulation (TMS).

Each of these techniques, along with several others, enables the experimenter, with varying degrees of temporal and spatial resolution, to identify which parts of the brain are active when a person is carrying out some cognitive task (e.g. naming a word). That is, they may tell us, provided various technical difficulties are overcome, where in the brain a process is taking place. It should, however, be noted that, in fact, there are many difficulties in going from the raw imaging data to reach this sort of conclusion; but for the purposes of describing the possibilities, we are assuming that these technical difficulties can be overcome (an assumption that, in fact, many would question).

Now, as noted previously in this chapter, knowing the spatial location of where a process is taking place (e.g. the left as compared with the right hemisphere) tells us nothing, in itself, about what is connected with what. But, nevertheless, imaging with good temporal resolution seemingly enables us to go beyond mere localisation. It provides a series of pictures over time, and hence enables the investigator to see in real time which parts of the brain are successively active when a person is doing a task such as reading a word and then pronouncing it aloud. Does this pattern of flow of activation tell us what is connected with what? Well, it does not in itself identify the operations of the units and therefore does not, in that respect, belie our previous claim that spatial location is irrelevant to the specification of the location of a unit (i.e. some particular operation) within a chain of units. However, if one theory predicts that the same units, whatever they may be (and regardless of whether the theories are coarse or fine grain), are employed in the production of two different behaviours – and, by contrast, another theory predicts no commonality of process – then the mere fact that a scan reveals a common spatial location would allow us to reject the latter theory and retain the former. Therefore, the technique could be of value.

Here is an example of how the technique might be employed in the way described above. One of the great debates in the study of language processing in the last century was concerned with the relation between syntax (which is concerned with the order in which different parts of speech – such as nouns and verbs – occur in a sentence) and semantics (concerned with meaning). When we hear a sentence, do we work out its grammatical structure using knowledge about word order alone, or can we use information about context and meaning to influence the construction of the grammatical structure (see Fodor, 1983; Harley, 2014)? Countless experiments, which involved making predictions about what behaviour should follow from a given environmental input, were carried out before people turned to imaging. But, given that imaging can be employed, consider one possible experiment that we might now be able to carry out. Suppose that by the use of imaging we could identify the regions of the brain that are used when computing the grammatical structure of a sentence or recognising a word; and suppose also that we could identify the regions of the brain involved in constructing the meaning of a sentence (or word). Then, it might be that imaging shows that, upon hearing a sentence, the activation of the brain of the listener proceeds from the auditory cortex to the word-recognition areas, to the grammatical processing area, to the sentence-level meaning area, with these stages of processing being temporally distinct. In such a case, we might conclude from this finding that the two processes are independent of each other. Suppose, on the other hand, we were to find that there are feedback connections from the sentence-level interpretation area to the grammatical analysis area, and that when we hear a sentence, these two areas are active simultaneously. Then we would conclude that the imaging data support the interactive view. And, indeed, such a finding has been reported in the research literature (Peramunage, Blumstein, Myers, Goldrick, & Baese-Berk, 2010).

It is also conceivable (we put it no more strongly than that) that there may soon be technological advances which will permit the measurement of inputs and outputs to operations in the brain without causing any tissue damage. Of course, even if such measures become feasible, the possibility of encountering difficulties in locating the inputs and outputs may arise. As noted previously, the procedure may not be anywhere near as simple as opening up a radio set and seeing what appear obviously to be inputs and outputs connecting blobs (which implement the relevant operation). If such problems concerning the relations between the anatomical structure of the brain and the operations it carries out obtain, then direct inspection will, at best, be greatly limited anyway. Also, difficulties will be more likely for coarse-grained analyses, since it is unclear how the different operations could be picked out since any one operation could be distributed over different parts of the brain (c.f. Lashley, 1929, 1950). In this context, it may also be noted that an effect of such a greater difficulty may be that the temptation to focus upon what is easiest to test (connectionist accounts) may come to dominate research activity, regardless of any comparisons with coarse-grained accounts that actually indicate which level of analysis should be pursued. We leave you to think further about the matter (which is all that we also can do).

At this point, the reader who has assimilated Part 1 of this book may raise the following 'objection'. As discussed extensively in Part 1, no measure is truly direct, in that variables other than the one the scientist intends to measure may influence the reading on the measuring instrument. There-fore, strictly speaking, inference is involved in direct measurement just as it is when one attempts to infer an internal mechanism only by studying the inputs and outputs of the black box as a whole. Nevertheless, we would sug-gest that unless some very peculiar inexplicable readings were registered by the instruments being used in taking our 'direct' measures (as in the Michel-son and Morley experiment discussed in Chapter 2), nobody is likely to query the readings. For all practical purposes, the readings given by what we shall continue to call direct inspection can be assumed to reflect only the value of the variable which the instrument was designed to measure.

A friend of ours pointed out that we should end this, rather complicated, chapter with some take-home message. Here it is. We have described a variety of approaches to the scientific study of understanding behaviour. But, which approach is best? As the reader should have gleaned from Part 1 of this book, the direction in which any science advances is not obvious before that advance actually takes place. Each scientist pursues what he or she believes to be the best approach, with many ideas falling by the wayside when some empirical or theoretical breakthrough constitutes a leap forward. But, unfortunately, which approach is going to be the most productive can-not be predicted beforehand. So we have no take-home message other than that we hope this chapter will assist some of you in deciding which approach seems, at present, to be the most promising one to take. Oh, and by the way, read the paragraph in this book that immediately precedes the conclusion of our final chapter (Chapter 13).

At the beginning of this chapter, we said we would examine two pos-sible approaches to the explanation of behaviour. We have now completed the first of these. In Chapter 7, we shall consider the second approach, that taken primarily by Skinner.

1   Typically, the cognitive psychologist takes the person whose behav-iour she wishes to explain as a mechanism consisting of operations which she does not directly examine. Yet she offers explanations of the behaviour which refers to those operations. Describe the char-acteristics of these explanations and the means by which cognitive psychologists test them.

2   In the attempt to understand behaviour, a typical approach within cognitive psychology has been to treat the organism as a black box, the mechanisms of which are inferred from input-output relations. Discuss whether it might be a better strategy to look inside the box, with the aim of discovering the mechanism by direct inspection.

3   Some researchers believe that the best way of understanding how the brain processes information from the environment is to build an artificial human brain. Do you think this approach is likely to be of value, and what difficulties would such a project face?

Test your understanding of Chapter 6

CHAPTER 7

Typical approaches in psychology

Skinner's functional analysis

In our introduction to Chapter 6, we suggested that one can identify three different approaches to the explanation of behaviour. We now consider the third of these, one associated primarily with B. F. Skinner, who took it in relation to the study of learning (Skinner, 1950, 1972); however, we believe it could be adopted in any area of psychology.

For Skinner, the goal of psychology is *the prediction and control of behaviour*. It is a practical goal: Skinner argues that if we can manipulate behaviour, we can better educate our children and raise better citizens. Skinner does not want 'understanding' in any sense other than it yields an ability to predict and control.

Given the goal of prediction and control, the discovery of laws relating behaviour to the environment, without any reference to the internal states or the operations carried out within the animal, is, according to Skinner, *sufficient* to achieve the goal. Given such a discovery, behaviour can then be manipulated, in some practical situation, by manipulating the environment. Hence, we have the law, for example, that when a response is followed by a reinforcer (reward), its frequency of occurrence will increase. The hope is that a small number of laws will have application in a large variety of situations, rather as Newton's three laws can be used to explain the behaviour of such apparently disparate events as the movements of the planets, the tides, and the movement of balls on a billiard table. Skinner believed he had discovered such laws of behaviour in the laboratory. Primarily, these concern association, reinforcement, extinction, punishment, and stimulus generalisation. Supposedly, just a few laws, plus the assumption that all behaviour is a result of learning, can be used to predict and control all behaviour. It seems to us that whether he is right in adopting this extreme assumption need not greatly concern us, for even if he is wrong, it is possible that a small number of laws may account for much of behaviour.

Skinner says that his approach is non-theoretical (e.g. Skinner, 1950). As indicated above, what he means by this is that he rejects any interest in formulating theories about what operations within the organism (the black box) link the environmental stimulus and the behavioural response. What he is doing is analogous to accepting Boyle's law concerning gases in an enclosed chamber ("pressure is proportional to temperature") without attempting to formulate a theory, such as kinetic theory, which would account for this law. Skinner observes a particular effect in a given situation, and extrapolates from this input – output relationship to formulate a law, this being that the observed behavioural effect will always occur in that situation. Thus, he interprets the effect only to the extent of going beyond the particular to the general. (See Chapter 2 for a discussion of laws and theories in general.)

Of course, in proposing behavioural laws, what Skinner advocates is, in a sense, theoretical in that it involves interpretation, not merely observation. For in proposing a law, Skinner has to correctly classify the input, the organism, and the behaviour if the law is to hold good. So, for example, he might show an effect for the rat, the pigeon, and the alligator, and then formulate the law: "All animals . . . ." Or he might observe that in a given situation, the behaviour of bar pressing increases when reinforced, and he formulates the law: "Whenever a *response* is reinforced . . . ." Or, even, "Whenever a press of a *two-inch bar* is reinforced . . . ." Generalisation from the particular always involves *categorising* the particular in some way (see Skinner, 1969, pp. 127–132). Choosing one category rather than another involves interpretation, in that incorrectly proposing that a particular case belongs to some category rather than another may lead to incorrect predictions. That is, that case may not have the same properties as the other members of the category to which it has been assigned. For example, drawing the conclusion that all animals behave in the same way as this rat may lead to incorrect predictions, in that fish may not follow the same law-like behaviour as the rat. Hence, it would not be true to say that Skinner is merely describing behaviour. (Consider here Toulmin's (1961, Chapter 4) historical example where cooking was thought to be the same sort of thing as the ripening of a seed, in that both were thought to be controlled by a goal – one of yielding a delicious cake, say, and a mature plant, respectively.) But in saying he is non-theoretical, Skinner used the term 'theory' in a technical sense, to refer to unobservable (i.e. theoretical) processes that can explain observed behaviour. Skinner rejects any consideration of the unobservable.

At this point it is appropriate to make clear something that is often not understood by psychologists and students, and therefore results in confusion. This is that, in rejecting references to unobserved inner events, Skinner not only rejects references to things that are, *in principle*, not open to test by observation (i.e. the objects of consciousness such as sensations – see Chapter 11 on consciousness). Almost all psychologists do this. He also rejects any concern with internal processes that are observable (e.g. neural activity), or theoretical processes (e.g. the operation of logogens) that, in having behavioural consequences, are open to test by observation. He rejects any study of these processes because he thinks that such study would be *unnecessary and unhelpful* in the prediction and control of behaviour.

OBJECTIONS

Even *if* we accept Skinner's goal of prediction and control, objections to the Skinnerian approach can be mounted. For the sake of argument, let us accept Skinner's goal and also his claim that knowing the laws of behaviour may be sufficient to control and predict behaviour. And, given this, let us now consider whether, nevertheless, it could be objected that the manipulation of behaviour by using only the laws to guide us is not the *best* approach for controlling behaviour (i.e. the best means of achieving his goal).

One objection is that if we knew the anatomical locations of the operations carried out within the 'box', we could control behaviour by action on the brain, say by chemical means or electrical stimulation, as well as by environmental manipulation.

But Skinner has a ready answer to this in that, although he would agree that action on the brain would yield control, it will never be a practical possibility on a large scale. And, by contrast, a manipulation of the environment – for example, means of reinforcement schedules – could be practiced on a large scale, say in the home or in schools. Furthermore, a case can be made that reinforcement schedules play a large part in shaping an individual's personality (see the chapter on Skinner's work in Hall, Lindzey, & Campbell's 1997 textbook on personality). More generally, in the context of a potentially wide and varying application of Skinner's work on a large scale, it is worth reading his utopian novel *Walden Two* (1948) or *Beyond Freedom and Dignity* (2002) to see how Skinner believes that what he advocates could be put into practice in the design of a culture.

It may be noted here that this reply of Skinner's is typical in that it is not a deep intellectual or profound answer that refers to some basic 'fundamental' principle – it simply focuses on what is best in practice, as befits Skinner's practical goal.

Another objection one might raise with respect to the Skinnerian approach is that it could be said that if we had a good theory, we could predict behaviour in novel situations, beyond that given by a mere application of the laws. By analogy, kinetic theory yields new predictions, such as Brownian motion, not derivable merely from Boyle's law. Hence, a focus on theorising could be the best way of realising Skinner's goal.

Again, the Skinnerian reply is a simple one. Yes, says Skinner, what you say is true, we could make predictions in novel situations. However, that presupposes that we do have a good theory. And, as yet, Skinner might say this is not the case. Moreover, in the meantime, before getting that theory, psychologists are likely to waste experimentation and thinking time formulating and testing a variety of different theories. Furthermore, according to Skinner, the history of psychology shows that this is the case. According to Skinner, psychologists spend much of their time setting up esoteric experiments to test competing theories as to how the brain works rather than seeking laws that will have application in practical situations. And, in consequence, no theory of cognition or learning has had much practical success. By contrast, Skinner claimed that the laws he discovered have been of benefit in practical application, for example, in the practice of behaviour modification and the application of teaching machines. Again, we think that Skinner would provide a down-to-earth practical answer (concerning the value of any one approach), perhaps something of the sort "The proof of the pudding is in the eating." But is his analysis of history correct? Let's consider an example of work in cognitive psychology and compare it with some of Skinner's work.

Throughout the history of psychology, theorists have raised the question, and sometimes assumed the answer, as to whether the processing of information in the brain (the black box) is carried out serially or in parallel. In particular, it has seemed to be a basic question as to whether search processes occur in serial or parallel. So, for example, when one views an object, is the perceptual representation of that object identified as an object of a particular kind (e.g. a tree) by a serial examination of the stored representations of all possible objects or, alternatively, by an examination of them in parallel? Similarly, suppose a person has the representations of various objects presently in short-term memory and that person is then asked whether or not another newly presented object is the same as any of those in memory. If the new object is identical to one of those in memory, is it identified as such by means of a serial or parallel process of comparison with those objects?

In 1966, Sternberg carried out a simple experiment concerning short-term memory comparisons. On each of a number of trials, a participant saw a series of one to six randomly selected digits, one following the other at intervals of 1.2 seconds. The participant was then shown a test digit and was asked to decide whether or not it was one of the digits previously shown. The participants were asked to respond as quickly as possible by pulling one of two levers, corresponding to "yes" and "no", with reaction times being measured. The results are shown in Figure 7.1. Essentially, upon being shown a

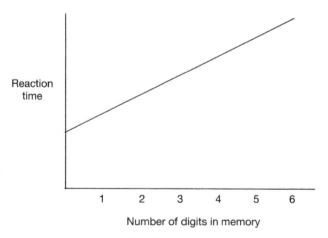

Figure 7.1 Results of Sternberg's (1966) experiment.

test digit, the participants' reaction times increased as the number of digits in memory increased, with no difference between "yes" and "no" responses. Sternberg identified several possible mechanisms to account for the data involving either serial or parallel processing; and, somewhat tentatively, Sternberg opted for one in which an internal representation of the test digit was compared serially to the digits in memory, with each comparison resulting in either a match or no match.

Over a period of what is now almost 50 years, Sternberg and a variety of other investigators have carried out a large number of further experiments with a variety of interpretations being offered for a growing body of data. Some of these interpretations have involved parallel processing and some have involved serial processing. And yet there still seems to be no clear indication of which one is involved – and no obvious scope for practical application of the results (see, for example, Donkin & Nosofsky, 2012).

Another question that psychologists have considered to be important refers to perception and imagery. The question is, does the information that is specified internally when we either perceive an object or imagine it take the form of a picture in the head? In the early 1970s, Kosslyn (1973) published the first of a number of experiments which suggests that information in imagery is indeed specified in the form of a picture. But although this claim may seem obviously true when judged by our introspections, others have suggested that the information is represented as a description in some internal language (e.g. Pylyshyn, 1973; Reed, 1974). In saying this, we should make it clear that the proposed internal language is not any language, such as English or Spanish, used in spoken or written communication with other people. Rather, it is a language that is (supposedly) used for communication in the exercise of a variety of capacities within the brain (memory, perception, imagery, and problem solving, for example – see Fodor, 1975). And presumably it is used in such communication by other animals also, for example, the rat. Well, again, surely this question, concerning the form in which information is specified in imagery and perception (and elsewhere) is a fundamental one, and as might be expected, numerous experiments have been carried out to determine the correct answer. However, yet again, this issue has still to be resolved (e.g. see Kosslyn, 1994; Pylyshyn, 2002).

In conclusion then, assuming these two examples are not atypical (see our final paragraph at the end of this chapter), Skinner would seem to have a point in claiming that much experimentation, even on basic issues, fails to lead to a resolution of those issues – thus making prediction in practice difficult – particularly in novel situations where having a theory would seem to be of advantage.

Now consider Skinner's contribution in the context of its practical application. Let's take a typical case of behaviour modification. Suppose we have a child who has severe learning disabilities. How can we teach them to tie their shoes? Let's assume that because of the severity of their condition, they lack the ability to follow verbal instructions, or copy the actions of a teacher. Well, we could just wait until they tie their shoelaces randomly, and follow this with a reward, making the prediction that having been reinforced, the behaviour will be more likely to occur on a future occasion. But the problem here is that the event of random shoe tying is extremely unlikely to occur by chance. So what is the teacher to do? According to Skinner, the desired behavioural chain, which constitutes tying one's shoes, should be broken down into component parts. This breakdown could begin by means of the teacher tying the laces almost completely and then waiting for the occurrence of the final step (pulling the laces say – which results in the tightening of the knot). The teacher would then wait for the child to (randomly) emit this behaviour, and then reinforce it. This procedure can be repeated a number of times until the child readily emits the response, the behaviour having been reinforced a number of times. Then, in the next stage of the process, the teacher ties up the laces to the penultimate step of partial completion (i.e. the step before tightening), and waits for the child to make those movements randomly. When the child has done this, the resultant outcome constitutes the stimulus for tightening the laces which the child has already learned. Reinforcement then follows just as it did previously. The training then continues in this fashion, working backwards to the beginning of the behavioural sequence, until the entire chain has been learned.

However, there are additional problems. First, although the behaviour may be broken down into component parts with each component being followed by reward, the reinforcing power of the reward is unlikely to be very great, and so it may take a number of presentations before the behaviour is established as a learned response. Such weakness in the effect of the reinforcer is consistent with what Skinner has shown in experiments concerning the effectiveness of reinforcement as a function of delay. As shown in Figure 7.2, a reinforcer is only very effective when it follows the response almost immediately (within about 0.5 seconds). So, for example, it has been

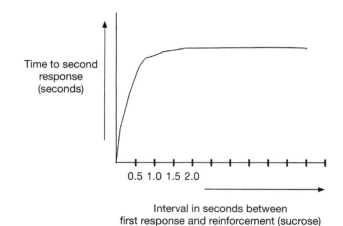

Figure 7.2 The effect of delayed reinforcement on learning.

shown that an injection of sucrose in the mouth of an experimental animal reinforces the pressing of a lever much more strongly than a delivery of sucrose in the food tray, which the animal ingests only when it reaches the food tray a few seconds later. However, it would seem inappropriate to use such immediate reinforcement in the case of a child. Nevertheless, we can draw on further experiments by Skinner to circumvent this problem. Suppose a rat is placed in a Skinner box and a buzzer is sounded at random intervals. And whenever the buzzer sounds, food is deposited in the food tray. Then, after a number of such trials, a lever is placed in the box such that whenever the rat presses the lever, the sound of the buzzer follows immediately. Given this setup, it is then found that the animal continues to press the lever a number of times. This shows that the buzzer has reinforced lever pressing, and such lever pressing will continue until the conditioned reinforcer (the buzzer) has lost its power to reinforce (no food is presented during this part of the experiment). The acquisition of such reinforcing properties by a formerly neutral stimulus (e.g. a buzzer) can be compared with a control in which the buzzer and food presentation are not correlated. In such a case, when the control animal first presses the lever, the probability with which it subsequently presses the lever does not increase, thus showing that the lever pressing of the first rat was indeed learned by being followed by reinforcing properties acquired by the buzzer. So applying this technique to the case of the child, into whose mouth we would be unwilling to inject sucrose, we could instead pair, say, a clicker (or buzzer) with a reinforcer in order to establish it as a conditioned reinforcer. Then, following this, the teacher could sound the clicker *immediately* following the emission of the response that the child has to learn.

Finally, there is the problem of how we get the child to emit any one component of the chain for the first time. In our example given above, it was noted that it would take a child almost an infinite time before they first emit by chance the behavioural sequence of tying their shoes. So it was said that what the teacher does instead is wait for the child to emit the final component of that behaviour (tightening the knot), in the hope that they would be likely to do this within some reasonable time. But in many cases, certainly this one, this hope would be unlikely to be realised – probably, it would be a very long time before the child emitted this behaviour randomly. So what can we do to improve matters? Well, it is well known that when a learned response is not followed by reinforcement, it extinguishes. However, something else of interest occurs also. In investigating the process of extinction further, Skinner discovered that extinction is not characterised simply by the probability of the response declining ultimately to zero, but also by a change in the character of the response. This change is called response drift. When the response is first non-reinforced, it tends to occur again exactly as it was learned; but then the movements that constitute the response begin to deviate from their original form. (It is almost as if nature has dictated to the animal that if the original response doesn't work, try variations of that response instead – perhaps the environment has changed slightly, and therefore some slight change in movement is required to get the food.) So how can we adapt this to the problem raised by waiting for the emission of tightening the shoelace by chance? Instead of insisting on *that response* occurring, we reinforce any movement that is in some respect more similar to it than doing nothing, for example, the child moving his hands towards the shoelaces. Following such reinforcement, this response tends to increase in frequency. However, rather than reinforcing it again, we now allow it also to extinguish. Thus, similar responses to the one desired tend to occur, for example, the child moves his hands even nearer to the laces. And so we reinforce that! Thus, by a reinforcement of gradual approximations towards the desired response, the child learns to emit that response (tightening the laces) in a relatively short period of time. And similarly, the same technique is used for the subsequent training of all the preceding elements, such that the end result is that the child can tie his shoelaces. The entire procedure we have described here is called *shaping* the behaviour.

Having concluded our description of the technique known as behaviour modification, it is worth making an additional final point. This is that, as understood by many persons, behaviour modification is merely the realisation of the principle that the way to modify behaviour is to reward it. And, as such, this appears to be just common sense – implying that Skinner has achieved little in relation to the technique. However, as we have seen, there are a number of important aspects of the technique which greatly increase the rate of learning. All these aspects have been discovered experimentally by Skinner and his followers, and the result is that the technique has been shown to be immeasurably more successful in establishing a desired behaviour (or behavioural sequence) than merely following that behaviour by a reward.

We have two final comments to make. The first is that, in this chapter we have taken the Skinnerian view, arguing that the attempt to discover internal mechanisms *has not* and *may not* yield a better outcome given Skinner's goals. We have done this partially in order to make Skinner's views clear. A less-partisan approach might (or might not) yield a different conclusion. Readers must decide for themselves where they stand.

The second final comment is merely one concerning nomenclature. Skinner calls his approach a functional analysis. He does this because he wants to examine behaviour as a function of the environment. That is, he wants to specify the relation between behaviour and the environment. Note also that the term 'function' is often used with a different meaning, for example, as referring to the purpose of a thing, as when talking about the design of a machine. (The function of a vacuum cleaner is to clean the floor.) Furthermore, the word is also used (incorrectly) in biology, as in "the function of the heart is to pump blood around the body." This usage is incorrect because organisms have not been designed – the natural selection that occurs in evolution has no purpose. So, beware of confusion: when you read about functional accounts, don't assume that the writer is necessarily writing about the Skinnerian approach.

1   Compare and contrast the approach to the understanding of behaviour taken by Skinner with the approach taken by cognitive psychologists. Might one of these approaches be preferred to the other, and if so why?

2   Skinnerians and cognitive psychologists seek different kinds of explanation for behaviour, arguably as a result of having different overall goals. Describe the different goals and the different kinds of explanation, and discuss whether the work of either (Skinnerian or cognitive psychologist) could be of relevance to the other.

3   Skinner claims that he is not a theorist. Discuss.

Test your understanding of Chapter 7

CHAPTER 8

Common-sense psychology and its implications

In daily life, we often give explanations of behaviour that we might call common-sense explanations. In this chapter, we shall describe the characteristics of these explanations. Then we shall ask whether these explanations are of the same sort as those usually put forward in science, for example, in courses on cognition in psychology. Finally, we shall discuss the consequences of our answer to this question.

COMMON-SENSE EXPLANATIONS OF HUMAN BEHAVIOUR

Often, in daily life, a person's behaviour is explained by showing how such behaviour made sense (was rational) given the person's desire to achieve a particular goal (purpose). For example, one asks, "Why did Jones cross the road?" and the answer given may be "Because he wanted tobacco (the goal), and believed there was a tobacconist's on the other side of the street." This answer shows why it was rational for Jones to cross the street, for if his belief were true, crossing the street would achieve that goal.

Consistent with what has just been said, common-sense explanations are unsatisfactory when they fail to show that the behaviour was rational (with respect to the person's goal). Suppose Jones were to say that he crossed the street because he wanted tobacco and believed there was a laundry across the street. This explanation fails to show that Jones's behaviour was rational; for, assuming that Jones's belief were true, the explanation would not imply that his behaviour would have brought about the goal. We either want to know more, for example, that Jones also believes that the laundry sells tobacco, or we conclude that Jones is mad (irrational).

Apart from being used in daily life, common-sense explanations (sometimes called folk psychology) are also given in history books and novels where they enable one to understand a person's behaviour and character. For example, historians ask: why did Henry VIII chop off Anne Boleyn's head? And an answer is: because he wanted a son, and believed that in order to bring about that goal, he would have to marry another woman. Thus, we see that common-sense explanations are pervasive in helping us to understand human (and sometimes animal) behaviour.

Note that a given explanation might be rational but false. So, for example, it might be suggested that Henry chopped off Anne's head because he collected skulls. In other words, an incorrect rational account of some action might be given, perhaps to deceive someone or as a result of making a genuine mistake in the assessment of motive. Thus, we see that rationality and truth are not to be equated.

Now let's consider common-sense explanation in more detail. In giving a common-sense explanation of a person's behaviour, one refers to the person as being in a state such as having a particular belief or desire. These states are often called *intentional states*. Following Brentano (1874), philosophers (e.g. Searle, 1979, 1983) characterise an intentional state as one that is *about* some *other* state. An easy way to understand this notion of 'aboutness' is as follows. When we say Jones *believes* that there is a tobacconist's across the street, we refer to a state of Jones (namely, the state of believing there is a tobacconist's across the street). However, included within the description of this belief is a reference to another possible state – in this case, the possible state of there being a tobacconist's across the street. The fact that Jones believes that there is a tobacconist's across the street is one thing; the fact that there is or is not a tobacconist's across the street is another thing – another possible state.

Some other examples of intentional states are as follows:

Jones *thinks* that there is a shop across the street.
Jones *desires* that there be a shop across the street.
Jones *intends* that he crosses the street.

INTENTIONAL STATES AND CAUSAL EXPLANATIONS

A number of questions may be asked concerning intentional states. One of these is whether or not explanations that refer to intentional states differ in kind from those that are ordinarily formulated in science. In other words, do explanations that refer to intentional states differ in kind from explanations which refer solely to causes and effects – one damn thing after another, as some wit described it. As we shall see, this question is an important one; but for the present, let's take its importance on faith and just try to answer the question and see where it takes us.

Consider a typical causal explanation. Suppose we want to explain how a car works. We might postulate a sequence of operations, beginning with the turning of the ignition key and ending with the movement of the wheels. And the sequence might, for example, include a piston – where a piston is defined as an entity which carries out the operation of compressing its input. Thus, the sequence that determines the behaviour of the motor car would include an input of petrol, compression of the petrol, and the output from the piston of vaporised petrol.

Now compare this with an explanation of a person's behaviour when that explanation includes a reference to the person's beliefs. Suppose Jones is standing on one side of the street, and he believes that just around the next corner, there is a shop across the street. In such a case, the belief, which partially determines Jones's behaviour, is defined in part by its being *about* something else, namely a shop around the corner. And, by analogy, we might say that the operation of compression is a compression *of* something else, namely the petrol. However, there is a fundamental difference between the two. The state of compressing petrol includes petrol as a component part; but the belief that there is a shop around the corner does not includes a shop around the corner as a component part. The shop around the corner, if there actually is one, has a location and existence in time that is independent of the belief. The belief is *about* the shop. In support of this analysis, note that if there were no petrol in the chamber, the operation of compressing petrol could not occur, whereas by contrast, if the shop did not exist, the belief that the shop is around the corner on the other side of the street could, nevertheless, explain Jones's behaviour of crossing the street to buy tobacco, just as it would if the shop did exist – the belief is the same in the two cases. Thus, we see that the two kinds of explanation do differ in kind.

Note that in a causal account, there is no place for describing the behaviour of something as rational or irrational. For example, there is no place for describing the behaviour of the car as appropriate or not with respect to realising the goals of the motor car, given its beliefs about the world. We do not ascribe goal-orientated behaviour, or beliefs about the world, to the car. And similarly, when we explain the behaviour of gases in kinetic theory by reference to particles, we do not imply that the particles are goal-orientated such that we could say that what they do, given their beliefs, is rational or irrational in the pursuit of their goals. Rather, we would (as in the case of the motor car) just describe a sequence of causes and effects with each event, for example, the movement of some particle, being following by some other event, according to the laws of nature.

Note also that not all human behaviour is explained by reference to intentional states. For example, suppose Smith, a university student, sneezes during a lecture she is attending. We ask why she sneezes. In some cases, the correct answer might be "She sneezed in order to annoy the lecturer." In such a case, we say that Smith intended something and that the intention was about sneezing (she intended to sneeze). And the behaviour was rational in that she had the goal or purpose of wishing to annoy the lecturer and believed that sneezing would accomplish this. On other occasions, however, a different kind of answer is required, for usually sneezing is not a purposeful action. In such a case, we have an answer such as "She sneezed because a bit of dust went up her nose." No reference is made to any goal or intending. Hence, the behaviour cannot be said to be either rational or irrational. Rather, the behaviour is explained as being a result of the laws of nature (a causal account), just like the behaviour of the motor car or the particles in kinetic theory. We are concerned here, however, only with behaviour for which an intentional account is appropriate, so let's continue to focus upon that.

CONSEQUENCES OF THE TWO ACCOUNTS DIFFERING IN KIND

Now consider the following question. Is an intentional account of some particular behaviour compatible with an ordinary scientific account of that behaviour? That is, could some behaviour which is usually explained by reference to intentional states be explained instead by reference to causal states, as in scientific accounts of other phenomena? This question is important, for if the two accounts are incompatible, and an account that refers to intentional states is true (implying that any causal account is false), then it must be that there is something special about living beings, such they differ *fundamentally* from inanimate processes (for which causal accounts can be given). In what follows, we attempt to determine whether or not there is this incompatibility.

Before proceeding, however, it might be noted that, apart from its intrinsic importance, any demonstration that there is such an incompatibility might be taken to shed light upon other issues concerning human beings. For example, many persons believe that human beings have free will. Hence, at least some of an individual's behaviour is thought to result from the exercise of free will rather than some cause. Therefore, the advocate of free will may see a link between free will and intentional accounts of behaviour. Perhaps they might argue that if human beings have free will, then any behaviour that results from the exercise of free will could only be explained by reference to intentional states as opposed to the causal explanations which explain other behaviour and the behaviour of machines (e.g. computers or robots). This argument would, incidentally, tie in with the fact that behaviour that is intended is often said to be voluntary, whereas non-intended behaviour, such as sneezing when a bit of dust gets in one's nose, is said to be involuntary. And then, it might be suggested that since we actually do use intentional accounts to explain human behaviour, this is evidence for the existence of free will. Thus, apart from its intrinsic interest, another reason for examining whether intentional and causal accounts of behaviour are incompatible is to see whether there might be a link to the possibility of free will.

Furthermore, another puzzle that might be linked to any incompatibility between intentional and causal accounts of behaviour concerns consciousness. As we shall see in Chapter 13, consciousness poses a problem for any ordinary scientific explanation of behaviour. However, if intentionality were shown to be incompatible with an ordinary scientific account, such that not all behaviour could be explained by causal processes, the possibility arises that there might be a role for consciousness to play in the determination of behaviour – even though, at present, we may have little idea as to what that role might be.

So, now let us consider whether the two accounts are incompatible. We shall argue that they are *not* incompatible. That is, there could be a mechanical (causal) account of behaviour consistent with an intentional account of that behaviour. Furthermore, even though an intentional account of some behaviour may be true, it would, at the same time, be possible to give an ordinary scientific account that is *sufficient* to account for that behaviour, without any reference to intentional states. That is, even intentional behaviour (e.g. sneezing in order to annoy the lecturer) can be explained by ordinary scientific accounts, without reference to intentionality. We will show this by re-visiting Tolman's (1948) account of behaviour discussed in Chapter 2, for we believe that it is of particular relevance in addressing this question. We will show that the internal states of a person or animal postulated by this single theory can be described in either of two different ways: they can be described either as intentional states (e.g. goals and beliefs about the world) or as cause-and-effect processes similar to those referred to in our account of the car above. From this it follows that even though an intentional account of a person's behaviour may be given, an ordinary scientific account can also be given – the two are compatible. Thus, the conclusion will be that our disposition to provide intentional accounts of behaviour does *not* imply anything fundamentally different about human beings as compared with inanimate objects.

Before we begin, we should make sure that we understand what a *representation* is, because our discussion will make use of this key concept. The notion is one we have described previously (see Chapter 2), but it may be helpful to remind you of it with a couple of examples.

1   A map of the London Underground represents (stands for) the actual London Underground. The purpose of the map is to enable one to find one's way around the Underground. Thus, one can *simulate* possible courses of action in the actual underground, finding out *what-leads-to-what*, by scanning the map, and then acting appropriately. In other words, with respect to what action a person might carry out, the map permits a person to plan ahead.
2   A set of black dots on a sheet of music represents a set of sounds.

In each of these cases, there is a correspondence between what is represented (the Underground, sounds) and the entities that stand for what is represented (e.g. a particular dot on sheet music stands for a particular sound). Hence, the representing entities are called representations.

THE RELEVANCE OF TOLMAN'S THEORY

According to Tolman, information encountered in the environment may be processed by the perceptual system and then stored on what Tolman called a *cognitive map*. The information is specified in neural codes that represent the environment, and can be used later to guide behaviour (Tolman, 1948).

As discussed previously in Chapter 2, Tolman developed the idea of the cognitive map in experiments on animal learning, and so we will illustrate and expand the idea by considering the performance of an animal in a T-shaped maze (see Figure 8.1). Suppose a rat has been allowed to run a T-maze for a number of trials, with food always being on the left-hand side and no food on the right-hand side. Tolman postulated that following such experience of the maze, the animal will possess a cognitive map consisting of a set of neural structures which correspond to the layout of the runway. As you should appreciate, the cognitive map is analogous to a map of the London Underground, where the latter shows what-leads-to-what in the actual London Underground.

As shown in Figure 8.1, each "location" on the internal cognitive map corresponds to an external location in the maze. When placed in the start box of the maze, these internal representations permit the animal to *simulate* possible courses of action in its head, without actually doing any of them (just as you might do when looking at a map of the London Underground). The simulation which has been found to link the starting point to the goal most effectively then causes behaviour that will bring about the corresponding sequence of states in the world (e.g. a succession of steps in the runway that result in the animal's arrival at the location where food was previously found).

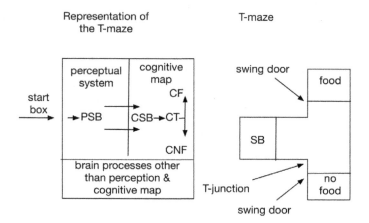

Figure 8.1 Illustration of relations between environmental input, the perceptual system, and the cognitive map. The following abbreviations are used:

SB is the start box.
PSB is the perceptual state in the rat that represents the start box (i.e. the animal perceives the start box).
CSB is the state in the cognitive map (memory) that represents the start box. The double arrow indicates that PSB matches CSB.
CT is the state in the cognitive map (memory) that represents the T-junction.
CF is the state in the cognitive map (memory) that represents the location where food was previously available.
CNF is the state in the cognitive map (memory) that represents the location where food was previously available.

Now, our strategy for using this theory to show something about intentional states will first be to suggest that accounts of behaviour that refer to representational states are *identical* to those that refer to intentional states. The two accounts just use different words to describe what is going on. The critical point is that in both cases, the description of any state, within the account, *includes some reference to another state*. For example, suppose the rat is in the start box. Then, with respect to Figure 8.1, we could say that since PSB represents the start box, the animal perceives that it is in the start box. And as the sequence CSB – CT – CF represents the path and food previously found in the maze, we could say that the animal *believes* that the start box leads to food, and so *expects* to find food if it takes that path. Moreover, we could say that when the rat actually moves out of the start box, it runs in order to reach the food, and that its *purpose* in running is to reach the food. So we shall accept from now on that the two types of account are identical (see also Searle, 1983, Chapter 1).

Now, given this identity between representational and intentional accounts, we shall proceed to show that Tolman's theory, and hence the common-sense intentional account, is compatible with an account of the animal's behaviour that involves no reference to other states.

We shall do this first by pointing out that one can describe the states within the animal without any reference to external states – as a sequence of connections, just as one could do in the simple case of a mechanical device such as a telephone switchboard or the more complicated case of a robot. To make this crystal clear, suppose that a neurologist were able to look at the (living) rat's brain in such detail that they could trace the chain of neurons that fire from a given external input to the behavioural response. If the neurologist could do this (and presumably there is no reason why, in principle, they could not), they would thereby provide a causal account of the animal's behaviour from sensory input to behavioural output. Note that the account would be complete in the sense that it would be *sufficient to explain behaviour* – there would be no gaps in the causal chain. Put another way, if one knew all the biochemical laws concerning the firing of neurons, one could deduce the behavioural output from the sensory input.

But then Tolman takes the stage and points out to the neurologist that the neurons and the connections between them correspond to (map onto) the structure of the external maze. Thus, Tolman gives *a different description* of the same neural structure, one that refers to the neurons as implementing a representation of the maze. And this description also could be complete in that no component of the representation of the maze is missing. *Thus, we have two different compatible descriptions of the internal structure that accounts for the relevant behaviour – a causal account and a representational account.*

By analogy, two different descriptions of a map of the London Underground could be given. By comparison with what the neurologist does, we could instruct someone unfamiliar with the London Underground (without them knowing that they were looking at a map) to trace out with a finger the connections between all the lines and circles on the page. This would be analogous to tracing out the causal chain in the rat. Alternatively, we could point to the circles and lines connecting them, and to the corresponding stations and lines in the London Underground, noting as we do so that the circles correspond to stations and the lines to track. Hence, we could formulate two different compatible descriptions of the drawing – either as a connective structure, in itself, or one corresponding to the London Underground.

Thus, we now conclude that since representational accounts and intentional accounts are identical, then intentional accounts also are compatible with ordinary causal accounts of behaviour (see also Dennett, 1987). *In short, we have shown that any one internal state can be described in either of two ways: either as an entity having causal consequences or as an intentional state.*

In passing, it might be noted that another way in which we might describe the two explanations is to say that, to give an intentional account provides the 'why' of doing something, where the 'why' is asking for the reason for doing that thing (e.g. in order to attain the goal of getting food); and to give the causal account is to give the means (i.e. the causal chain) by which the something is done.

THE TWO CASES OF SNEEZING, AGAIN

We are now in a position to understand the difference between the two cases of sneezing described earlier. When the student sneezes in order to annoy the lecturer, that is a goal-directed action requiring the use of the cognitive map to determine what-leads-to-what (hopefully sneezing will lead to annoyance on the part of the lecturer!). Hence, an intentional explanation, referring to intentional states, is appropriate. And, by contrast, sneezing because a piece of dust went up the student's nose is not a goal-directed action. It requires no use of the cognitive map. Of course, in both cases causal chains are involved in the production of the behaviour – the difference being that these include the causal properties of representational states in the one case and not in the other. (In the latter case, we might say that the response is merely a reflex. But if so, we should be clear as to what we would mean by that. We would not mean that the behaviour is caused as opposed to not being caused when it is not a reflex. Rather, we would mean only that its occurrence does not involve the cognitive map.)

VERBAL UTTERANCES

It might be suggested that what has been said is fine in the case of rats. But what about human beings? They are able to talk about their intentional states. For example, the student can readily explain why she sneezes in the lecture. Well, in outline at least, we can, with the addition of appropriate machinery, see how a person may make various verbal utterances. For example, the vocal apparatus, in the case of a human being, could be connected to all the relevant circuits shown, so that each unique state in the cognitive apparatus evokes a unique verbal utterance. Hence, Smith may utter the words: "I desire . . .", "I believe . . .", etc. These utterances would, of course, be caused by antecedent events. From the point of view of a causal analysis, they do not differ from the utterances made by a robot, or even the sounds produced by a gramophone reflecting the indentations (corresponding to words) on a record.

SOME MORE EXAMPLES

We have shown, using a number of examples, that the variety of different intentional states to which one may refer in giving common-sense explanations can be mapped onto a simple theory which postulates an internal cognitive map of the world. We shall now provide some further examples. Our reason for doing this is simply to show you that it seems that all intentional states can be mapped onto a mechanism in this way. The list really is impressive. Also, since some of you may be tired of reading about rats, we will now assume that the relevant animal is a human being.

Suppose Jones is out for a drive one sunny day. He is bowling along and suddenly an old lady steps into the road. Jones puts his foot down hard and *tries* to brake. But the brake is stuck. Jones realises that this is what has happened because the proprioceptive feedback from the contracting muscles in his leg, indicating that his leg is not moving, does not match that predicted by the cognitive map. Hence, although Jones tried to brake, he *failed* to do so and is *surprised* that he has failed. But then, perhaps with an extra strong push, he *succeeds* in braking, and *knows* he has succeeded, not only because the car screeches to a halt but because the proprioceptive stimuli generated by the movement of the leg matches that *expected*. Alternatively, suppose that the additional push also is ineffective, and Jones hits and kills the old lady, a result which was not *intended*, not *foreseen*, and not *deliberate*. And now suppose, in order to extend our illustrative cases, a different scenario. Suppose Jones ran over the old lady *on purpose* (just as the rat ran on purpose down the maze, *anticipating* food at the end). This act, being guided by predictions made from information previously encoded in Jones's cognitive map (when a fast-moving car hits a person, it is likely to kill that person), was *deliberate*.

SOME POSSIBLE OBJECTIONS

One possible objection to the preceding illustrations is that an observer of Jones's behaviour does not ordinarily have access to the cognitive map in order to draw the distinctions discussed. That is true. Ordinarily, like any other person, they have access only to Jones's behaviour. But it was not our intention to suggest that the distinctions made by an observer are ordinarily made on the basis of a direct knowledge of the cognitive map. Rather, they are made by making inferences as to the internal state of a person on the basis of what a person, such as Jones, does and says. In this respect, making inferences is like making inferences in carrying out cognitive psychology (e.g. inferences concerning logogens or short-term memory) – although, of course, as has been shown in this chapter, the inferences are made in relation to a different sort of account of behaviour.

A second objection concerns consciousness. It might be said that our analysis of intentional states seems to be sound as far as it goes, but that we are wrong to exclude any reference to consciousness. Consider, for example, the case of expectancy. Often when we expect something, our expectancy is a conscious one, and it might be suggested that some reference has to be made to this expectation. However, there is an expectancy of the sort that one has when one is, for example, walking down the stairs, and one's foot falters at the bottom. In such a case, one might then say "I thought there was another step." In this case, you do not consciously expect another step beforehand, and the above analysis explains it in full (since any question pertaining to consciousness does not arise). A similar case may occur in relation to beliefs, some of which one is aware of and others of which one may never be aware of. Now, given that we are sometimes aware of our intentional states and sometimes not, we would suggest that whether one is consciously aware of an intentional state seems to be a question that is separate from the question as to what intentional states are (i.e. states that are about some other state – the absence or presence of another step, for instance). You may or may not accept this. In Chapter 13, we shall see that the question of whether consciousness plays any role in accounting for behaviour is an extremely difficult one to answer. Therefore, until we address the topic of consciousness, we think it best to put aside any queries concerning a possible role for consciousness in intentional action. Then, when we have considered consciousness in some depth, the reader can come to his or her own conclusions as to whether there is anything we could say about consciousness that would challenge or add to the 'consciousness-free' account given in this chapter.

SUMMARY

Given all that has been said, it seems that sequences of causes and effects are sufficient to account for all the distinctions made by a theory which invokes intentional states. Hence, there seems to be no requirement that intentional states be invoked in order to explain behaviour that ordinarily we would explain by reference to some intentional state. Hence, there is no reason to suppose, on any grounds concerning intentionality, that human beings and other animals differ fundamentally from inanimate objects.

WHY DO WE LIKE INTENTIONAL ACCOUNTS?

As we have seen, although we frequently refer to intentional states in order to explain human behaviour, for example, in daily life, history books, and novels, it is not necessary that behaviour should be explained in this way. In principle, we could simply refer to the causal chains that determine a person's behaviour. Why, then, do we find it desirable to point out the 'aboutness' nature of the states? One reason is that it enables us to see, from an evolutionary point of view, why these particular causal chains evolved. Selective pressures in nature favour the selection of any causal chains that constitute a model (representation) within the animal's head. They favour this because such a model permits planning ahead and problem solving. If we considered the causal chains in isolation, without realising their mapping, then by definition we would not realise that the neural circuits within us constitute a model of the world.

Another reason why we like intentional accounts is related to the preceding one. The fact that our brains have evolved such as to embody a cognitive map as a way of coping with the world means that we think about our own behaviour in terms of intentional concepts. Therefore, it is plausible that, as a social animal, we find it advantageous to think about others in the same way – enabling us to predict and understand their actions (see Dunbar, 2004, pp. 120–121). By contrast, we ordinarily have no understanding of ourselves in terms of the cause-and-effect sequences that presumably account for the understanding we do have. And, incidentally, perhaps that is one reason why some students who study psychology find it difficult to think in terms of chains of causes and effects as a possible alternative to thinking in common-sense terms. The difficulty is not one that is analogous, say, to understanding the behaviour of a car by reference to the causal interactions between a large number of individual atoms as opposed to the fewer number of levers and pistons formed by those atoms. As we have seen in the course of this chapter, causality and intentionality differ in the kind of explanation they provide – to that extent, analysing another person's behaviour solely in terms of causes and effects is alien to our natural thinking about that behaviour.

1   Describe the difference between explanations of human behaviour that refer to intentional states (e.g. Searle, 1983) and explanations that, in science, are ordinarily used to account for the 'behaviour' of inanimate objects. Discuss the significance of the difference.

2   Suppose two students are attending a lecture. They both sneeze – one because a piece of dust went up her nose, the other in order to annoy the lecturer. Describe the difference between the explanations that would be given to account for the two cases. Could a single type of explanation be used to account for both cases?

3   Describe and compare intentional and causal accounts of behaviour. Are the two compatible?

4   Discuss the view that scientific accounts of behaviour, such as those put forward by psychologists or neurologists, might someday replace the explanations of behaviour given in novels and history books.

Test your understanding of Chapter 8

CHAPTER 9

Free will and determinism

Before we begin our analysis of free will and determinism, some comments are in order concerning the relation of this chapter to Chapter 8. In Chapter 8, we argued that common-sense explanations of behaviour, referring to a person's intentions, plans, and purposes, are *not incompatible* with a causal account of such behaviour. And we then went on to describe, in outline, a causal account of that behaviour. However, something we did not mention was that intentional behaviour is, contrary to any causal account, usually believed to be generated by the exercise of free will. This belief can be illustrated, for example, by the common use of language which implies that the behaviour is voluntary when it is carried out on purpose (with the cognitive map being involved) and involuntary when it is not (as shown by the two cases of sneezing). Given this, the reader may ask why we did not consider this assumption in Chapter 8. For example, in our description of Jones running down an old lady on purpose, we made no mention of the possibility that Jones would thereby *be held responsible* for his action, and that he was to *blame* for what had occurred. We made no reference to such notions because we wanted to separate the question of whether common-sense explanations are *compatible* with causal explanations from the question as to whether, even if a causal account were shown to be possible, it might not be correct because we actually have free will. Effectively, we assumed the operation of causal processes in order to address the question of compatibility. By contrast, in the present chapter we shall be more open-minded, asking what we mean by free will and whether it might be possible to show that we do or do not have it. Clearly, if it could be shown unequivocally that we do have free will, then the rationale for writing the last chapter (Chapter 8) would no longer obtain. But, as we shall see, things are not as simple as that.

Nevertheless, some of what will be said in the present chapter may remind you of what was said in Chapter 8. However, the issue of whether or not we have free will is a difficult one to address, and so in order to avoid complicating matters, we strongly urge you, in reading the present chapter, not to relate it to Chapter 8, except insofar as we shall now take the possibility of causality for granted. We suggest that you keep the two chapters in separate mental compartments, at least until you have independently assimilated what is said in each.

Let's begin by making clear what is meant by saying that a person has free will. In exhibiting purposeful, intended behaviour, it is commonly believed that a person exercises choice; for example, John *chooses* to cross the road to buy tobacco. And, in saying that John chooses to cross the road (say), we imply that he *could have done otherwise* – he could have chosen not to cross the road (see Campbell, 1951). This definition of free will (the person could have done otherwise), as well as being intuitively obvious, also has the advantage that it fits comfortably with the circumstances under which we believe we can hold a person responsible for his actions. We hold King Alfred responsible for burning the cakes; and we say he *deserves* praise or blame for his action – why? Because we think he could have done otherwise. And by contrast, we do not hold the stove responsible for its actions when it burns the cakes. We don't praise or blame the stove for doing what it did; we don't say it deserves to be punished. We just fix it. We do not hold it responsible because we do not believe it could have done otherwise. It behaved in the way that it did because causal processes determined its behaviour.

In passing, it may be noted that, although we are saying that it is a *necessary* condition for a person to have free will that they could do otherwise, we are not saying that they could do otherwise is a *sufficient* condition for them to have free will. There is a theory in physics (quantum mechanics – see Chapter 5) which states that very small particles may behave randomly. That is, they could have done other than they did in fact do. Yet no one suggests they have free will. So what is it that is missing? We suggest that in order to say the person has free will, we also have to include the idea that what they do, they do for a particular *reason* to achieve a certain goal (and no one suggests that quantum particles behave as they do in order to attain some goal). However, in this chapter, we are going to focus only on the requirement that a person could have done other that they did. And we shall simply assume, without discussion, that if a person can choose to do one thing rather than another, he does it in relation to some goal.

As mentioned above, the suggestion that human beings are able to choose what they do, that they have free will, is often contrasted with the suggestion that the behaviour of other entities is *determined*. To say that the behaviour of some entity (e.g. Alfred's stove, a billiard ball) is determined is to say that it must behave as it does (it could not do otherwise). For example, billiard ball A strikes billiard ball B *causing* B to move off, implying that B *could not have done other* than move as it did. (Do not get confused here by our interchangeable use of the words 'caused' and 'determined'. Perhaps some event could be determined and not caused – we are unsure about this – but for our purposes, the two words can be used interchangeably.)

Note that the assumption that we have free will is made implicitly within normal social intercourse in daily life. We intend to do most of the things that we do. Moreover, individuals are blamed and praised for intended actions; and, as pointed out above, moral judgements are made only when it is assumed that the relevant action was undertaken by choice. Similarly, in criminal law, behaviour is viewed differently according to whether it is intended or not. Intended behaviour is assumed to result from choice, whereas behaviour that is not intended is assumed to be caused/determined. Compare running down an old lady on purpose to get her money with accidentally running her down. We hold the perpetrator both morally and legally responsible in the former case, but not in the latter. The assumption that we have free will is pervasive in the judgements we make in political, legal, and everyday life. We shall examine this social aspect of free will in Chapter 10.

Consistent with what we have just said, many psychology students have a belief in free will, quite independently of anything they have learned in psychology. Why is this? Perhaps it is simply because they realise that there is a difference between an act of theirs when they intend to carry out that act (sneezing to avoid the lecturer) and when they do not (sneezing because a piece of dust went up their nose). But as we saw in Chapter 8, the difference between these two could be accounted for solely by reference to different causal chains. We shall therefore dismiss that intuition here and, in this present chapter, restrict ourselves to asking whether scientific investigation, perhaps by psychologists or neurologists, could show whether or not humans have free will.

It may be best to begin by dismissing one reason sometimes given by psychology students for believing that human beings have free will. The reason concerns the rationale for the use of statistical inference carried out in experimental psychology. In carrying out their experiments to discover laws of behaviour, psychologists typically compare groups of subjects and use statistical inference to discover whether the independent variable has any effect. Yet, physicists typically do not do this. For example, in his experiments on gases, Boyle may have heated just one instance of an enclosed gas, measured the change in pressure and, on that basis, proposed his law relating pressure to temperature. (Well, perhaps he replicated his discovery a number of times, but certainly there was no testing of groups with statistical inference.) So what's the difference between psychology and physics that warrants statistical inference in the first case but not in the second?

We might think that the difference is that human beings have free will, and therefore that in some particular situation, some may choose to do one thing and others something else. Hence, we might think that we need to use statistical inferences to draw a conclusion concerning what the participants in an experiment choose to do on average. However, this is not so. Rather, as in physics, it is, we believe, assumed by most psychologists that human behaviour is determined; but unlike physics, there is, in addition to the independent variable, often a large number of uncontrolled variables of which an experimenter is ignorant (e.g. genetic differences, previous experience) which may affect behaviour. Statistical analysis enables the effects of these to be taken into account in assessing whether the independent variable has an effect.

For clarity, the behaviour of an individual person can be compared with the cooling of a cup of coffee. We ask a physicist how long it will take for the coffee to cool. They reply,

> Goodness me – I don't know – it all depends on a variety of factors, each of which would have to be measured and their effects calculated; for example, its initial temperature, the surface area of the cup, the thickness of the cup, the thermal conductivity of the cup, and wind speed.

Thus, the rate of cooling of the coffee results from a number of variables, just as the behaviour of a human being does. However, in the physics laboratory, unlike the psychology laboratory, almost all these variables other than the one being deliberately manipulated (the independent variable) can typically be held constant. Hence, there is no need for statistical analysis.

For additional clarification, consider also the hypothetical case of identical twins with exactly the same environmental history, including their experiences in the womb, and now in exactly the same situation. Then we would predict that they would behave in exactly the same way – wouldn't we?! That is, we assume that human beings are governed by the laws of nature just as inanimate objects are. (Perhaps we should note here that we realise that for any pair of real twins, there must be some difference between them; but of course we are merely describing an idealised thought experiment, of the sort often practiced by philosophers, in order to illustrate a particular point.)

In conclusion then, the use of statistical inference in psychology is not relevant to the question of whether or not we have free will.

In the present context, it is also worth returning to Skinner's contribution to psychology. Skinner made an important contribution in addition to that discussed in Chapter 7. Guided by the dictum "control your variables and order will emerge," Skinner constructed what others have called the Skinner box. The Skinner box is 'merely' a strictly controlled environment, within which the behaviour of an animal, for example a rat or a pigeon, can be studied. So, for example, in the case of a pigeon, the bird is placed inside a chamber (the Skinner box) of about 50 squared centimetres that has a disc at about pigeon height on one wall which, when struck (say by pecking), activates a micro switch. This in turn can, by the use of other equipment outside the box, be used to activate other consequences within the box, for example, the delivery of food to a food tray. For example, Skinner might programme the apparatus in such a way as to vary the colour of the disc (pigeons have colour vision) many times over the course of an experimental session, with each colour constituting the occasion for the occurrence of food delivery following a particular pattern of responding (pecking at the disc) peculiar to that colour. Thus, whenever the disc turns blue, the bird may, for example, immediately peck at a slow rate, say, if a slow pecking rate has been previously reinforced when the disc was blue; and whenever the disc turns green, the bird pecks at a high rate if a high pecking rate has been previously reinforced when the disc was green – and similarly at other rates for other colours. It is most striking to observe such behaviour. By means of a one-way observation panel, one can see control in action – so to speak. That is, the behaviour is seen to be strikingly orderly in relation to the only variable which changes within the bird's environment (the colour of the disc). Thus, we see clearly that the presumption that behaviour conforms to lawful relations to the environment is again supported. At the time of writing, we have found several video recordings on the Internet which illustrate the degree of control permitted by use of the Skinner box, and we believe that psychology students will find them to be of interest.

DO LAWS OF NATURE IMPLY CAUSALITY?

Having established that, in general, psychologists assume that human behaviour is subject to law, we shall now consider the big question of whether lawfulness implies causality. In their experimental work, psychologists are in the business of discovering laws of human behaviour; and it is often supposed that if such laws can be discovered, then this, in itself, will show that the behaviour is the result of causal processes (i.e. that behaviour is determined) rather than being the result of an exercise of free will. But, is it true that the occurrence of behavioural laws does imply the operation of causality? We shall now address this question.

Let us consider the question first by reminding ourselves of what a law is. In using the term 'law', we mean a constant (regular) conjunction that always obtains between particular states of affairs. An example is as follows. Suppose there are two billiard balls on a table. Then, the following law might obtain: "If all variables are held constant other than the movement of Ball A, then whenever Ball A strikes Ball B (the antecedent state of affairs), there follows a movement of Ball B from its state of rest (the subsequent state of affairs), whereas when there is no movement of Ball A, there follows no movement of Ball B." (See Frank, 1957, Chapter 12.)

Now consider the relation between laws and causes. Suppose it is a law that whenever Ball A strikes Ball B, then B moves. Ordinarily, without reflection, we would probably suppose that whenever this sequence occurs, Ball A caused Ball B to move. In his groundbreaking book *A Treatise on Human Nature* (1739), Hume said that our psychological makeup is such that from the observation of the constant conjunction between the antecedent and subsequent states of the balls, the impression is formed within our minds that one state must lead to the other. (That is, B could not have done other than what it actually did: that is, it was caused to move as it did.) However, most importantly, Hume then went on to say that this impression could be misleading, for actually we cannot legitimately conclude that any causal process is at work. Thus, Hume denied that, from the demonstration of a law, one can justifiably conclude that the one state of affairs causes the other. Hume made two points in support of his claim (see Ayer, 1980; Salmon, 1998, p. 193).

First, Hume pointed out that although it may be a fact that whenever Ball A strikes Ball B and B then moves off, that fact does not *logically imply* that B had to move off. Instead, it is logically possible that on each occasion when A struck B, B merely happened to move off. Thus, we see that the existence of a law does not logically imply determinism. To make sure this is clear, let us remind ourselves what is meant by 'logically possible'. A husband has to be married, because that is part of the definition of being a husband: it is part of what we mean by 'husband' that the person concerned is married. Hence, we cannot even suggest that it might just so happen that all husbands are married – for it would be contradictory to say that any man is both a husband and unmarried. It is simply not logically possible that there could be a husband who is unmarried. By contrast, in the case of the billiard balls, it is not contradictory to suppose that A could strike B, and that on one or more occasions of such a strike, B *could have not moved off* – even if, in fact, it always does move off.

Note that this is not a point about the fact that an infinite number of occasions are required to establish a law (see Chapter 2). In order to appreciate this, suppose, for illustration, that we could and do observe an infinite number of occasions when A strikes B and B moves off. Then we still could not conclude that on any one of these occasions, B had to move off as it did. For it is always possible it could have done otherwise, but it just so happened that it did not.

Second, Hume asked whether there is anything we could *observe* that would show us that Ball A caused B to move off. And his answer was 'no'. All we can observe is that Ball B moves off (and no occasion when B does not move) – there is nothing else to be observed – there is no observable causal link. And, given that there is nothing to observe which would show us that causality is involved, perhaps Ball B *merely happened* invariably to move off. (See Hempel, 1958, pp. 170–176; Hospers, 1997, Chapter 5.)

In response to this point, you, the reader, might say that you accept that causality can neither be logically implied nor shown by observation; but surely it is reasonable to interpret what is observed by postulating that a causal process is involved? After all, what is the alternative? You (the authors of this book) have said that perhaps it just so happens that B moves off every time. What does this mean? Surely if it occurs *every* time, then either it must be caused by the antecedent event, or it occurs randomly; and since it occurs every time, it is very unlikely that it occurs randomly. (A student made this point to one of us several years ago.)

We accept this response, but point out that you are confidently opting for the causality interpretation here because there is no plausible alternative. You will see shortly why we make this point. For the moment, we want to reiterate that Hume has at least shown that the demonstration of a law does not necessarily mean that causal processes are involved (neither logic nor observation can be used to demonstrate causality), and therefore, when we come to consider human behaviour, we are licensed to consider whether there might, unlike the case of billiard balls, be a plausible interpretation of regularity other than that of causality.

LAWS OF HUMAN BEHAVIOUR: CAUSALITY OR FREE WILL?

Now let us return to the consideration of human behaviour. Psychologists assume that there are laws of behaviour (if you think this is not so, ask yourself why they do experiments), and they are in the business of demonstrating them. And as we have previously pointed out, it is often thought that any demonstration that human behaviour conforms to laws implies that such behaviour is caused, and hence that humans do not have free will. But, as we have seen, this is not the case. As Hume showed, using the example of one billiard ball striking another, to say that two events are related by a law (regularity) does not *in itself* mean (imply) that the antecedent event causes (determines) the consequent event. Moreover (unlike the case of the billiard balls, perhaps), in the case of human beings, there is an *alternative interpretation* ready to hand, one other than that of chance. The alternative explanation is that in any single instance, the person may have chosen to do what they did.

Is this alternative plausible? Perhaps we can rule it out as implausible in a manner similar to the way we ruled out chance in the case of the billiard balls. In that case, it was argued that it is implausible that chance alone would yield a relation between events such that one event always followed the other. Similarly, it is often thought that a person who exercises free will would necessarily sometimes do different things in the different repetitions of some antecedent situation. But that need not be so – the case is very different from that of chance. Indeed, it is highly plausible that, even though the person could do otherwise on any one occasion in a particular situation, he or she would always freely decide to do the same thing in repetitions of that situation. Consider, for example, Smith catching a train at 9.00 a.m. every morning – the train which takes her to her place of work. The behaviour is so regular that we can even predict it. And Smith could explain such an ability to make correct predictions by saying "Of course, I do it of my own free will, every morning." Given that Smith wants to arrive at work on time, of course she chooses to catch the train each day. She could do otherwise, but naturally, she does not. So the occurrence of behavioural laws *per se* implies neither an absence of free will nor its implausibility.

In summary, in the case of human beings, the discovery of laws of behaviour (and the ability to predict behaviour) is consistent with behaviour being either caused or being a result of the exercise of free will. Therefore, any psychologist who argues that the discovery of laws of human behaviour implies that we do not have free will is wrong.

Given that there is no other way of testing which of the two accounts is the correct one, it follows that the distinction between could not have done otherwise (must/cause/determinism) and could have done otherwise (free will) is a *metaphysical one*. To say that the distinction is metaphysical is to say that it is not possible, either by logical analysis or observation, to show which interpretation is the correct one.

Nevertheless, the results of observation may provide a *plausible* case for opting for one of the two possibilities. Although the discovery of laws of behaviour does not, in itself, point selectively either to determinism or free will, it might be possible to argue that if behaviour conforms to certain kinds of laws, it is more plausible to assume an operation of cause and effect rather than free will. In order to illustrate this, consider further the previous case of Ms Smith behaving in a regular (lawful) way. If it could be shown that Ms Smith's behaviour could be deduced from the laws of biochemistry or physics when these are discovered to hold *independently* of processes outside the brain, it would then be hard to argue that the laws of behaviour are merely those which result from the person's decisions. Why should a person always happen to decide what the laws of chemistry would predict? As far as we can see, there is no plausible way in which the advocate of free will could argue that any chosen behaviour should always be the same behaviour as that predicted by these laws. They are going to have to say that it just happens to be a coincidence. Is this plausible? And moreover, even if they could argue that it is plausible, the opponent of free will could say that any reference to free will that is made in providing an explanation is redundant. (Note again, however, that it is not redundant as to whether an action is judged to be moral or immoral, for if the concept of moral behaviour is to be applicable, free will must be assumed.)

Of course, contrary to what we have just supposed, it might be discovered that known biochemical laws are not sufficient to explain behaviour. In that case, it might plausibly be claimed that something else brought about a person's behaviour – and what could that something else be? – possibly an exercise of free will.

Our conclusion is that no conclusion is forced upon us, although the data might, with some justification, convince us one way or the other.

Test your understanding of Chapter 9

1 Describe the concepts of free will and determinism, and discuss whether or not the psychologist who seeks to discover laws of behaviour is committed to the view that behaviour is determined.

2 It has sometimes been suggested that because psychologists evaluate their data by the use of inferential statistics, the behaviour of individual human beings must be unpredictable, and therefore that humans may have free will. How would you respond to this argument?

3 Describe the concepts of free will and determinism, and discuss the relevance of empirical studies of behaviour and the nervous system to the question of whether human beings have free will.

CHAPTER 10

The possible impact on social institutions (the legal system) if we relinquish our present disposition to believe in free will

In Chapter 9, we made the point that research psychologists are, among other things, in the business of discovering laws of behaviour, and insofar as they are successful, this may seem to indicate that persons do not have free will. However, we then saw that Hume showed that any discovery of such laws would not actually imply an absence of free will. Behaving always in the same way in a particular situation is consistent with either a person being caused to do as they do or with the person exercising a choice as to what they do.

Nevertheless, as may have been apparent in your reading of Chapter 9, Hume's argument is subtle, and even well-educated and thoughtful members of the general public may not appreciate it. Hence, as even more laws of behaviour are discovered, they may come to *believe* that causality governs human behaviour. Usually, perhaps, the work of scientists affects the public only with respect to technological developments; but in the case of the study of human behaviour, any advance in understanding that leads to the loss of our belief that we human beings have free will would have a more general impact, relating to the way we humans see ourselves. In this chapter, we shall consider the possible impact in society of such a change in the present belief that we have free will, to the belief that we do not have free will, and in particular the impact upon one of our social institutions – the legal system.

Before we begin, however, let's look at some previous cases where science has had an impact, not limited solely to scientists, on the way humans view themselves and their place in the world. The number of such cases has not been great, and it could be argued that although science has by means of its technological application led to enormous changes in our material well-being, it has had little effect upon the conception we have of ourselves. There are two notable exceptions, however.

The first of these concerns the relation between the earth and the rest of the heavens. In the time before Copernicus, Kepler, and Galileo (in the 16th and 17th centuries), it was assumed throughout European society that the earth was a stationary body lying at the centre of the universe. Thus, the sun, for example, was thought to travel round the earth, as did all other heavenly bodies, such as the stars. This belief was in harmony with the view that man was the primary creation of God, with what remains of the universe being of secondary concern. Man was literally at the centre of the universe.

However, as a result of the work of Copernicus, Kepler, and Galileo, it came to be believed instead that not only does the earth travel round the sun, but it is also merely one of a number of planets to do so. In terms of social impact, this belief led to an erosion of the idea that it is man that is of primary importance in creation.

The publication of Darwin's *On the Origin of Species* (1859) led to another more recent example. According to the theory of evolution, man evolved from other animals. Hence, man was thought no longer to be qualitatively different from the other animals. Previously, it had been thought that, unlike animals, man had been created in the image of God, with the possession of a soul. It became more difficult to argue this as the basic idea of evolution became generally accepted in society.

It is also worth noting that Freud, in his *Introductory Lectures on Psychoanalysis* (1917, pp. 284–285), stated that science has dealt three "wounding blows" to humanity's conception of itself, with rational man at the centre of the universe: the Copernican revolution, the theory of evolution – and the third and most wounding blow being dealt by Freud himself, with the discovery of the power of the unconscious.

So, given this background, we shall now consider the possibility that the discovery of laws of behaviour by psychologists, and other scientists who study various aspects of human beings, may persuade many members of society that we do not have free will (even though, as we have seen, an absence of free will is not actually implied by such laws). And given this, we shall consider some of the possible changes in our view of human beings that may result. In particular, we examine the consequences for our understanding and justification of our (Western) legal system, as exhibited in the rationale and justification for the sentences passed on offenders against the law.

CRITERIA FOR IMPOSING PUNISHMENT ON OFFENDERS

Let's consider the criteria for imposing punishment on lawbreakers in Anglo-US law (see Hart, 1961). Initially, we shall describe these without defending them or trying to justify them. In giving our description, we shall assume it has been established by the court, typically a judge or jury, that the defendant did actually carry out the actions of which they are accused, and hence the only remaining question is how they are to be treated.

Essentially, the treatment of an offender will fall into one of two general categories, depending on the mental state of the offender. If the offender's mental state meets the criteria specified on the right-hand side of Table 10.1, they are sentenced to some form of punishment. On the other hand, if their mental state does not meet these criteria, then, as shown on the left of the table, they fall in the category we have labelled as 'excused'. That is, they are deemed not to be liable for punishment. (The category shown on the left is therefore defined by the absence of the mental state specified in the

Table 10.1 Treatment of an offender following conviction.

Excused from punishment	Liable for punishment
Instances where liability does not apply since conditions in the right-hand side column do not hold, either in part or entirety. For example:	The offender knew what they were doing and anticipated the consequences of their action. They intended to do what they did with the aim of achieving the lawbreaking consequence.
1 *Insanity* – The offender thought that the person they killed was the devil. This is a case of the offender not anticipating the consequences of their action. The offender thought they were killing the devil, whereas they were actually killing a human being.	The treatment of the offender is one of punishment typically involving pain, imprisonment, or other consequences normally considered unpleasant.
Treatment of the offender: the offender may undergo treatment for their condition and be confined to a psychiatric hospital to prevent a repeat offence; but there is no intention to punish them for what they did.	
2 *Accident* – The offender was within the speed limit, and an old lady stepped into the road. The offender did not intend to kill the old lady.	
Treatment of the offender: none.	
3 *Loss of control* – the offender was driving their car and had a blackout without warning, killing an old lady.	
Treatment of the offender: they may have their license taken away in order to prevent a repetition of the offence, should they be disposed to have blackouts in the future; but there is no intention to punish them.	

category on the right.) We have not specified either category in great detail because we assume that, as a presumed member of Western society, the reader will be already familiar with both of them. Readers who wish to read more about the categories may consult the work of Hart (1961), from which Table 10.1 is derived.

In summary, an offender is classified into one of two categories, these being determined by the offender's mental state, with their subsequent treatment being dependent upon the category into which they fall.

This classification may be compared with the policy of *strict liability*, a policy which stipulates that a breach of the law is always punished, with no excusing conditions. Thus, there is no division into categories; and so, for example, the treatment of an individual who has killed another is the same, regardless of whether the killing was accidental or deliberate (murder).

A consideration of cultures other than our own suggests that a policy of strict liability is only rarely, if ever, adopted. Some form of classification similar to that shown in Table 10.1 is the norm. So, for example, the rights and duties of the Roman citizen, which were displayed in the Roman Forum, about 450 BC, included the following section (taken from Lewis, 2003, p. 29):

> Any person who destroys by burning any building or heap of corn deposited alongside a house shall be bound, scourged, and put to death by burning at the stake provided that he has committed the said misdeed with malice aforethought; but if he shall have committed it by accident, that is by negligence, it is ordained that he repair the damage or, if he be too poor to be competent for such punishment, he shall receive a lighter punishment.

Admittedly, the classification used by the Romans does not exactly correspond to that described in Table 10.1, but its correspondence is sufficient to show a basic distinction between actions based on malicious intention as deserving punishment, and those that do not.

It seems apparent, then, that most people, not only in our culture but in others also, reject strict liability as undesirable, presumably because they believe in the appropriateness of the categories. Hence, one can ask what rationale underlies the dual classification and subsequent treatment of the offender that they find so appealing.

Two different possibilities, moral culpability and deterrence, are commonly proposed as a rationale for the dual classificatory system. Moreover, as far as we are aware, it is not stipulated in any document or tradition that either one of these rather than the other is the one to which persons working in the legal system should subscribe. We shall now consider each of them.

Moral culpability

While reading Table 10.1, the reader will probably have assumed that the offender whose mental state is described in the right-hand column has free will (i.e. in any action they carry out, they could have done otherwise). However, for later reference, let us note that the possession of free will by the offender (or any other human) is *not* implied by any statement within that column. However, in describing the *first rationale* for the categorisation, we will *assume* that the agent (and human beings in general) do have free will. Given this assumption, here is a summary of the rationale. Punishment is considered to be *deserved* by offenders who acted of their own free will with evil intent ('mens rea'). And, by contrast, excusing conditions apply when the offender could not help doing (was not *responsible for*) what they did; hence, it would be unfair to punish them: the offender does not deserve punishment.

Of course, you might question whether what the offender (supposedly) *deserves* is actually used in legal practice as a justification for punishment, as we are claiming. It seems to us that the courts do indeed use the notion of deserving punishment as a rationale (although sometimes mixed with deterrence – see below). For example, some offences are described as heinous or wicked. As Hart notes (1961, p.101), Lord Justice Denning asserted that "In order that an act should be punishable it must be morally blameworthy. It must be a sin." Also, we do not punish children for their evil behaviour – unlike adults, they are not considered to be responsible for their actions. A court may decide that there should be some attempt to *rehabilitate* a child or *correct* their behaviour, of course, but the aim in doing this is not one of administering a deserved punishment.

Deterrence

We now suggest that the reader looks again at the right-hand column of Table 10.1. As we have noted already, nothing in that column logically implies that the offender has free will. It could be, as often assumed by psychologists, that the attitude and behaviour of an offender were caused, as, presumably, would be the rest of their behaviour (see Chapters 8 and 9). Thus, a determinist would necessarily reject moral culpability as a rationale for how offenders should be treated, and instead consider what categorisation might be justified consistent with a belief in determinism. A rationale, based on the assumption that human behaviour is determined, was clearly articulated by Bentham in the 19th century. Bentham held that we should punish (i.e. make the offender pay a penalty) only to deter future behaviour of the same sort – not because the offender *deserves* punishment.

A rationale based on deterrence, allied with a generally humane approach towards offenders, yields the same, or at least very similar, classification as a rationale based upon moral culpability. Consider the case of a sane offender as compared with that of an insane offender. Bentham believed that to punish an offender who is sane would deter both that person and other sane persons from committing the offence again. He believed this because he thought that sane people would anticipate that same consequent punishment when considering committing the crime on some future occasion, and so be inclined to desist from committing the same offence. Therefore, on these grounds Bentham believed that punishing a sane offender is justified. However, to punish an insane offender would deter neither the insane offender himself nor other insane persons, for the reason that an insane person, unlike the sane person, would not be capable of realising the consequences of his action (i.e. punishment). Therefore, on these grounds, it makes sense to place an insane person in an 'excused' category on the grounds that this is the most humane action to take. Bentham also believed that to punish the insane would not deter a sane person, for, according to Bentham, a sane offender would believe that the judges would realise that a sane person was not insane, and so could not avoid punishment on these grounds. Therefore, there is also no reason to punish the insane on the (invalid) grounds that punishment would deter the sane. Of course, one might ask whether Bentham's claims are correct, but attempting to answer this question would require a much more substantial analysis than we could offer here. So we will simply accept that a classification of how to treat offenders according to what yields deterrence, allied to a humane approach, would correspond closely, if not entirely, to a classification that is based on the assumption that persons have free will.

In summary, there are two more or less corresponding ways of justifying the system of classification shown in Table 10.1 – one which assumes that human beings have free will, and the other that they do not. In practice, one of the justifications is employed, and sometimes the other; and sometimes it is not clear which one is being used, or indeed whether the justification employed is some mixture of the two. Often, which one is being used is not stated in court. This may not be surprising given that they correspond so well in relation to what they prescribe for the treatment of an offender (punishment or no punishment). Such a correspondence means that the courts do not have to ask themselves which rationale they should employ in order to determine their decision.

THE POSSIBLE IMPACT OF PSYCHOLOGY UPON THE LEGAL SYSTEM

Now let us suppose that in years to come, the impact of future advances in the social sciences on the more educated members of society will be to persuade them that human beings do not have free will (a plausible supposition, we believe). What will be the consequences? One consequence is that, in relation to Table 10.1, the rationale for the classification based on moral culpability collapses. See Greene and Cohen (2004) and Farah (2010, Part 5) for more discussion of this point.

And then, what would be the consequences of such a collapse? It all depends on what behavioural laws the psychologists will have discovered. At present, when relatively few behavioural laws have been established, persons in society make assumptions about what those laws are, with little reference to the work of psychologists and other scientists. For example, they typically assume that human beings behave in the way that Bentham assumed (for example, that a spell in prison will deter an offender from committing further offences). Now if these assumed laws are actually correct (i.e. they match the ones discovered by the scientists), there may be very few consequences of relinquishing our belief in free will. The reason for this is that the way an offender should be treated is then usually, and perhaps always, the same (e.g. a spell in prison), according to a rationale of either moral culpability or deterrence. Putting an offender in prison is held to be both a punishment that is deserved and a deterrent. So it does not make much practical difference which rationale we assume. Hence the educated elite, who would be the ones most likely to hear of and be influenced by new discoveries, can offer the Benthamite rationale for the present practices of the court, without much concern for what the 'ordinary' citizen believes concerning whether or not human beings have free will.

But suppose that psychologists discover that the actual laws are not as Bentham thought, so that the two forms of treatment, one based on moral culpability, the other on deterrence, would no longer be the same. Suppose, for example, that the best deterrent is found to be giving the offender a big piece of apple pie. (We exaggerate here, but it is quite possible that laws will be discovered which imply that giving a caution, or otherwise treating the offender gently, is the best way of reducing offending.) Then, what will be the reaction of those members of the general public who still believe in free will? They will not be happy! We already see tensions among different members of society in the way offenders have been dealt with in recent years. More generally, an argument could be made to the effect that, at present, members of society are willing to leave the administration of justice to 'the judicial system'. They are willing to do this because they believe it to be, in general, just and fair, based upon sound principles. These principles are: punishment of those offenders who are blamed for what they did, and merely trying to prevent the recurrence of offending when an offender has been judged not to be blameworthy. But if this system were to be rejected by the judiciary and replaced by one, say, in which a piece of apple pie was given to an offender because that had been shown by psychologists to be the best deterrent, many members of society might lose confidence in the judicial system. And they might then begin taking matters into their own hands, such that we would see lynch mobs and vigilantes on the streets, or at least some general unhappiness and non-acceptance of the rulings announced by the judiciary.

In summary, it has been argued that although the two ways in which we presently justify the classification shown in Table 10.1 presently correspond in what they imply concerning the treatment of an offender (e.g. the offender may be sent to prison), this may change – depending upon what laws of behaviour are discovered by psychologists in the future. It is possible that changes may occur which would generate a rejection by many people of the 'sentences' handed down by the judiciary.

COMMENT ON POSSIBLE CHANGE IN PUBLIC ATTITUDE

We shall now comment upon the likelihood of a change in public attitude as a result of advances in the social sciences. In the preceding discussion, it has been assumed that those educated individuals who reflect upon and make decisions within the judicial system will lose their belief in free will under the impact of argument and the discovery of laws in the social sciences. This assumption, it will be recalled, was made even though the demonstration of such laws does not actually imply the absence of free will (see Chapter 9). However, as we also suggested, it is likely that the vast majority of even the educated public will not have been exposed to Hume's arguments concerning the problems associated with the identification of causality, and therefore may take the demonstration of laws to imply that human behaviour is determined.

However, alternatively it may be that (regardless of whether or not they are aware of what Hume said) educated individuals will never lose their belief in free will, whatever the advances in psychology and the other sciences. There are at least three reasons why this may be so.

First, in most day-to-day circumstances, psychologists may never be able to predict or control behaviour, because in practice there are so many uncontrolled variables that govern it. Yes, we may be able to show control in the Skinner box, but most people have had little occasion to see this in practice. Hence, they have little reason to question free will on the grounds of demonstrated laws in artificially well-controlled situations. They see others only behaving in the world outside, and since so many variables are then affecting behaviour, that behaviour may appear to be unpredictable.

It is of interest to note that the cooling of a cup of coffee discussed earlier is similar to the apparently non-determined behaviour of people in the world outside the well-controlled laboratory. Because there are so many variables that affect such cooling, a physicist would not be able to predict the rate at which it would occur in practice. But we already accept that the cooling of coffee is a causal process, whereas we do not already accept that human behaviour is determined: in fact, we reject it – in that we assume free will. Hence the questioning of free will, engendered perhaps by a realisation of the possibility of a determination by uncontrolled variables operating causally, may not even come to mind.

The second reason why educated individuals may never lose their belief in free will pertains primarily to those among them who have studied psychology. It may be that, like many of us, students 'compartmentalise' their knowledge, believing, in their case, that what they learn about human beings in lectures and practical sessions is one thing, whereas the way people are in 'real life' is another. (It is unclear, however, what the grounds would be for holding such a belief.)

The third reason why educated individuals may never lose their belief in free will is it may be very difficult to give it up, regardless of any argument or evidence to the contrary. Consider the following.

Suppose that for one reason or another (the reasons need no longer concern us), many educated people, familiar with science and having the belief that the behaviour of human beings is subject to natural law (just as billiard balls are), state with genuine conviction that they do not believe in free will.

Nevertheless, we suggest that the beliefs which people genuinely think they have, and espouse in intellectual argument, may not reflect their actual beliefs, at least as shown in the decisions they make. The two may differ, and we fail to realise this because, at present, the category distinction that in criminal law implies that an offender should be punished or excused can be given a rationale by reference to either free will or the deterrence advocated by Bentham. Hence, the person who professes to be (and indeed believes himself to be) a determinist can happily go along with the offender being given 20 years in jail, advocating this on the basis of deterrence without considering whether their professed belief in determinism does actually reflect their deepest beliefs. Thus, it is possible that their "intellectual" resolution of the issue actually runs contrary to an implicit belief in free will which they do not even realise they have. But what if we suppose (in what philosophers call a thought experiment) that the two 'rationales' do not coincide in their implications with respect to how the offender should be treated? Then we would be forced to confront our actual beliefs as a basis for deciding how to treat the offender.

Such a thought experiment can be illustrated by asking a person who claims to believe in determinism the following question.

Suppose a person kills another intentionally, saying, for example, "I did it for fun" or "I did it in order to gain money." Suppose also that empirical investigation by social scientists has discovered that the best deterrent (marginally better than any other, say) is to shoot any one person randomly chosen from the population. Would you, Ms or Mr Determinist, have any reason to reject the latter in favour of specifically selecting the offender?

As the reader should appreciate, the purpose of our setting up this hypothetical scenario is to force the listener to confront their actual beliefs, rather than the beliefs they sincerely profess to hold. In order to do this, we formulated the conditions of our thought experiment so that:

1   A determinist can have no grounds for selecting the offender as the one to be shot, rather than selecting a person randomly.
2   A person who believes that people have free will does have grounds for selecting the offender.

Hence, if the person who claims to believe in determinism finds that they would select the offender, this surely means that, in fact, their actions are those of a person who believes in free will. That is, their *real* belief, previously unrecognised by them, is that human beings have free will. The beliefs they have arrived at by using a process of reasoning are not those that they actually hold and act upon. In a sense, they have been deceiving themselves.

Note that if you think that the hypothetical situation we have described is not such as to unequivocally test whether the person believes in determinism or free will, then we should try to modify it so that it does; for only then can we see whether the person's answer tells us what in practice their beliefs actually are.

We have asked a number of persons who profess a belief in determinism to undertake a process of self-examination in order to answer the question we have posed, and have found that most, if not all, say that they would select the offender as the one to be shot. This result, we suggest, shows that, whatever reasons have previously been accepted by a person for not believing in free will, it is often the case that the person comes to realise that their selection is actually based on a belief that it is the perpetrator of the crime who *deserves* to be shot (rather than some random person). It is very difficult to give up one's belief in free will!

Finally, we should perhaps again remind the reader that nothing we have said here implies either that we do have free will or that we do not. Rather, it shows something about our 'belief' in free will, namely that it is very hard to give it up, even when intellectually we argue (correctly or not) against it.

OVERALL CONCLUSION

It seems to us that it is unclear whether or not the social sciences will have a sufficiently large impact on society to erode a general belief in free will. But if it does, many of our social attitudes and institutions may be subject to considerable change, perhaps with conflict between those who believe in free will and those who do not.

Test your understanding of Chapter 10

1   "It is as illogical to condemn a man for stealing as to condemn him for contracting influenza" (Butler, 1872). Discuss.

2   The belief that human beings have free will is pervasive. Describe some ways in which this is exemplified in our social interactions and institutions. Consider whether the work of psychologists might cause a change in this belief.

CHAPTER 11

The problem of consciousness

We begin this chapter with an admission of defeat, but one of which we are not ashamed. The admission is that although we believe that we adequately explain why the occurrence of consciousness is puzzling, we fail to present any really convincing solution to the puzzle. Accordingly, we do not expect you to provide a solution either. It is enough that you come to appreciate the magnitude of the problem. If you do provide a convincing solution, we will consider nominating you for a Nobel Prize.

First, let us remind ourselves of the sort of events that are studied in science. Science is the study of those events that can be learned about by observation, that is, by using our sense organs (e.g. our eyes) to pick up information about the world. For example, a person may observe the event of a swan swimming in the village pool. As was explained in Chapter 2, such an event (one open to observation by the eye or by means of instruments) is called a physical event.

The biological sciences, including psychology, make the assumption that the behaviour of animals, including human beings, can be explained entirely by physical processes. So, for example, it is assumed that, in principle, and perhaps actually sometime in the future, we shall have a complete account of behaviour of the following sort depicted in Figure 11.1. What do we mean by complete account? As illustrated in Figure 11.1, we mean that for any environmental situation, one could, in principle, trace a chain of physical events (e.g. the activation of a series of neurons), each causing an activation of the next, with the final outcome being the evocation of behaviour. Following an injury to the knee (say), such behaviour could include utterances such as "I am in pain" or, upon looking up at the sky, "I have a sensation of blue." To give a simple but good analogy, one could compare the process with playing a gramophone record where the placement of the needle on the record causes a sequence of vibrations which results in the sound "I am in pain."

In order to avoid confusion (there is plenty of scope for that later) we should perhaps add a note here concerning cognitive psychology: as we saw in Chapter 6, cognitive psychologists typically do not observe neurons (they do not open the box). Rather, they postulate the occurrence of internal operations that can explain the results of experiments showing various effects of environmental inputs upon behaviour. But, nevertheless, their belief is that these operations are implemented by physical processes such as neurons.

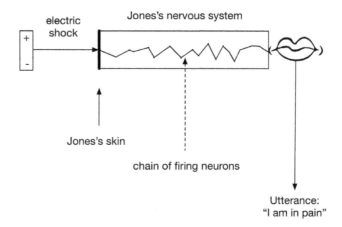

Figure 11.1 A diagrammatic explanation of behaviour, predicated on the assumption that behaviour is determined solely by physical events.

We do not think we need consider this point any further in what follows, for as far as we can see, it is not relevant to the issues that arise concerning consciousness.

CONSCIOUSNESS

Suppose that what we have said above were to be presented to a class of first-year psychology students. In response, one of the students might suggest that there is something additional to the physical processes depicted in Figure 11.1, namely the pain itself; and, moreover, that this seems to play a part in the production of behaviour, for example, making a visit to the doctor, or crying for help.

In response to the student, the materialist/scientist/neurologist/cognitive psychologist denies that there is anything additional, and may offer any one of three analyses to dispel that idea. In each of these analyses, it is claimed that the student is making a conceptual error.

The first of the three analyses was proposed in a classic book written by Ryle (1949). The form of Ryle's argument enables one to understand clearly how one could suffer under a misconception concerning the concepts one is using, and hence seemingly encounter an intractable problem. Ryle begins by agreeing that, unlike the examples of raising one's arm or sneezing, being in pain is not a behavioural event. (Also, it is not a physical result of the firing of a neuron – see later discussion.) Hence, it may appear to be an additional 'ghostly' non-physical thing that accompanies or produces behaviour, for one might ask, what else could it be? But Ryle has an answer. He suggests that to classify it even as an event is what he calls a *category mistake*, analogous to the following. A novice might think that in cricket, the team is a thing that is additional to the players, the ball, the wickets, and so on; but it is not: rather, it is merely a way of classifying these things (the totality of the players on one side is called a team).

Now, Ryle claims that a similar analysis obtains with respect to the relation between mind and behaviour. For example, he suggests that knowing French is merely a disposition to speak French (behaviour) when appropriate – for example, when in France. Thus, to say that a person knows French is merely a way of saying something about their behaviour. It is not something that exists in *addition* to behaviour. Upon learning of this analysis, the first-year psychology student agrees that it is plausible. So far, so good.

But what about pain or any other sensation? Ryle offers the same analysis in this case as well. According to him, being in pain merely refers to a disposition to exhibit any of a particular set of behaviours when appropriate (e.g. uttering "ouch" when pinched). But the student says no – in this case, Ryle's claim is implausible with respect to either pain or any other sensation. And again, he insists that pain is something that is additional to behaviour. So, according to the student, Ryle has taken a case where we might readily admit a category mistake: initially accepting that we tend to classify the ability to understand French as some ghostly state within our minds, and then showing that such a thought includes a category mistake, and therefore dispelling the problem of how there could be such a ghostly state. But in extending the argument to pain (and other sensations), the student says that Ryle goes 'too far'. Based on their own experience, the student is confident that being in pain is not merely a disposition to exhibit certain behaviours (such as crying or shouting "ouch").

The second possibility has been in vogue more frequently, but the claim seems to us to be of the same sort as that made by Ryle (in that our concern about consciousness is unwarranted since it merely reflects a category mistake or something very similar to it). The claim is that consciousness (for example, being in pain) is an *emergent property* of the nervous system. An emergent property is a property that is inherent in the lower-level description of some event but not readily derivable from it. It is usually taken to be a complex process that arises from the interaction of a number of relatively simple interactions. A good example is the apparently complex flocking behaviour of birds, which can be demonstrated to arise from the application of a few simple rules which imply that each individual bird keeps an equal distance from its neighbours and flies in a direction determined by their average direction. At first sight, there is a tempting analogy to be made between the flocking behaviour of birds (for example) and the action of neurons. The birds can be considered to be identical to each other in all respects other than their spatial configuration, with their disposition to respond differentially being dependent upon their position within that configuration. Similarly, it may be assumed (for simplicity) that all neurons are identical, with the disposition of each to be active being dependent upon its position within a neural configuration. And, just as the emergent behaviour of the flock is dependent upon the configuration of the flock, so consciousness is presumed to depend upon the configuration of the neurons. (Our guess is that most persons do not believe that consciousness would emerge as a result of the stimulation of a single neuron lying in a petri dish.) Moreover, just as different configurations of identical birds account for flights of the flock in different directions, so different configurations of identical neurons may account for different experiences, such as redness or pain. On the face of it, the analogy seems exact.

However, there is a fundamental difference: the analogy is actually far from exact. The difference concerns the readily answered question of whether or not an emergent property is anything other than the physical relations between the relevant individual objects (e.g. birds, neurons). And it seems clear that in the case of the birds, the answer is no. Put another way, one can deduce the emergent property from the spatial location of all the individuals, and that property (e.g. the birds are strung out in the shape of an arrowhead) is measurable by instruments (i.e. it is a physical property). The same is true also of other so-called emergent properties, for example, the crystalline structure of some materials. That is all there is to it: for, by contrast, we do not *observe* our sensations. Thus, as far as the student is concerned, there is no mileage whatsoever in exploring further the idea as stated earlier: the student believes that pain is something *in addition* to being in a particular physical state, and no matter how we re-route the neurons in Figure 11.1, the student will still say, "No, being in pain is not measurable; it is not subject to observation."

Perhaps it could be argued that the higher-order property that emerges in the case of some physical structures might not be deducible from the properties of the elements – perhaps it emerges in some seemingly magical fashion. But still, the basic point that invalidates the analogy remains: if the higher-order properties are subject to observation, they are, by definition, not something in addition to the physical – they are physical!

The third analysis that the lecturer may propose is perhaps less clearly related to the one suggested by Ryle, but is nevertheless a category mistake (or at least reminiscent of one). The claim is that pain and the firing of certain neurons is the same thing. So, for example, a psychologist who adopted this position might say that it is legitimate to identify being anxious as some particular activity in the neurons of the limbic system. But the student replies by referring to a paper by Jackson (1982). In this paper, Jackson makes it clear that the activity of neurons and sensations are not the same thing. He considers the case of Mary, a hypothetical neurologist, who knows all that can be observed about the nervous system and then, having led a sheltered life, experiences pain for the first time, exclaiming that she now has knowledge of something that she never previously knew existed. Thus, pain is something additional to the physical (see also Nagel, 1974).

So, at this point we are going to side with the student. There is something additional to the physical. It may be noted, however, that, speaking as authors who have had a science-based education, we do so reluctantly. We have great sympathy with those which have put forward suggestions, such as those described above, as to how one might be able to deny that there is something in addition to the physical. The advance in our scientific understanding of the world has been great over the last several centuries – indeed, so much so that our knowledge of it may soon be complete (without any obvious gaps). Yet nowhere has there been even a hint of something non-physical except in the case of human beings and perhaps other animals. This seems very odd. Surely it must dispose us to thinking that somehow we are making a mistake in admitting something additional. Yet, as we have seen above, no mistake has yet been convincingly demonstrated. In fact, one could argue that attempts to find the supposed error seem quite desperate. Our conclusion, therefore, is that there is something additional to that which can be observed.

THE CHARACTERISTICS OF SENSATIONS

We shall now put aside our consideration of what the relationship between physical events and sensations might be and consider what we can say about sensations in their own right.

It has been argued above that we do not identify sensations (e.g. pain) by means of observation. (If we did, pain would, by definition, be a physical event.) But given this, how then is pain identified? We now explore this issue. The result of our exploration might not be entirely satisfactory, but, neverthe-less, may be illuminating in revealing previously unappreciated differences between physical events and sensations.

First, let us remind ourselves of the characteristics of physical events. As discussed extensively in Chapter 3, the identification of some event by observation implies the identification of that event by means of its effects. In Chapter 3, we saw this initially in cases when conventional instruments are used to identify (measure) a property of some object; but we also saw that it obtained in identification by 'the naked eye'. This point is illustrated in Fig-ure 11.2, a figure previously shown in Chapter 3. Essentially, the perceptual

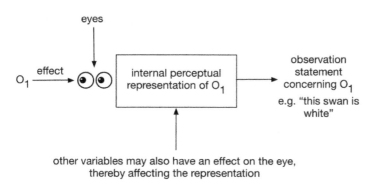

Figure 11.2 Repeat of Figure 3.3: schematic diagram of the eye as a measuring instrument.

system is an instrument, such that what is being measured is identified by means of its effect on that system. And, just as with conventional instruments, a consequence of this is that errors in identification are possible. In a sense, what we do is infer the value of the property we are looking at from the output of the perceptual system, with the possibility of error resulting from the possibility of other variables also influencing that output (the reading on the instrument).

We shall now describe two characteristics concerning the identification of sensations.

Direct apprehension

It is a characteristic of any sensation, for example pain, that it is apprehended *directly*: we do not gain knowledge of a sensation by means of its effect, either on the eye or by some (other) measuring instrument. Russell (1912, Chapter 5) was perhaps the first to express this clearly, coining the expression "knowledge by acquaintance" for what we have called direct apprehension. Unlike the case of observation, no process analogous to inference is involved. If you do not immediately accept that this is so, then ask yourself: what is it that you infer the properties of your sensations from? Surely the answer is nothing – we do not identify sensations by means of their effects (or anything else); rather, we identify them directly.

Not subject to error

We discuss here a characteristic that results from the fact that we apprehend our sensations directly. This characteristic is that we cannot make *errors* of the same kind that we have been discussing in the case of observation. Consider, again, the sensation of pain. Could one be in error as to whether or not one is in pain? Well, one could make an error when one calls a sensation one is having by an incorrect name, say, by calling pain something else, or by calling some other sensation 'pain'. However, this is not the kind of error that is of interest here. Rather, the question is whether one could make an error of the kind that in observation comes from the measurement being indirect – the error occurring as a result of the reading given by the perceptual system being affected by variables other than those being measured. For clarification, with respect to the possibility of error, the contrast between the physical and the mental may be summarily illustrated by the following. Suppose, on looking at a swan on the village pond, a person reports "There is a white swan" and "I am having a sensation of whiteness". But now suppose, to give a crude example, that a chemical is injected into a person's eyes which changes their response to the light reflected from the swan. Then the person might report "There is a blue swan" and "I am having a sensation of blueness". In this case, there is an error in the report of the swan's colour, but none (of the same kind) in the report of the sensation. Moreover, in the latter case no error of the same kind as that which occurred in reporting the colour of the swan could be made.

The following objection is sometimes raised against the claim that a person cannot be in error concerning whether or not they are having a sensation, let alone a particular sensation. Consider a footballer fully engaged in an important match. He falls over and gashes his knee. It hurts, but the footballer plays on, and in playing on, feels no pain; but when he stops playing, he again feels pain, exactly as before. Under circumstances such as these, it is sometimes argued that he was in pain all the time but had insufficient capacity to attend to the pain, and hence did not feel it, because all his attention was focused upon playing vigorously, and thinking about what to do next.

This case suggests that one could be in error about whether or not one is in pain, since supposedly the footballer was in pain but not aware of it. However, there is a counter argument which indicates that this is not so. Suppose we could completely expose the brain of a living person without damaging it (as depicted schematically in Figure 11.1). And suppose that the person felt pain only when tissue damage activated some particular sensory neuron, and that neuron in turn also activated, in competition with other neurons, some centre which directed attention to that neuron. Suppose, then, that the competition from the other sources became so dominant that the sensory neuron failed to activate the attention centre. Would it make sense to say that the person was still in pain, even though they could no longer feel pain? The answer is no, for the reason that the supposed pain would have no properties. It would, so to speak, be a *something that is a nothing* (a phrase we coined in homage to the philosopher Wittgenstein [1953]). Pain, in order to be pain, has the property that it is necessarily felt (apprehended). If, contrary to this claim, you think that a pain which is not felt would have one or more properties, tell us what they are!

If what we have said about sensations being apprehended directly and without error is correct, it not only elucidates the differences between physical events and sensations, but also, in pointing out what we recognise these differences to be, on the basis of our knowledge of ourselves, provides further support for the claim that the two are indeed different.

THE RELATIONSHIP BETWEEN SENSATIONS AND PHYSICAL EVENTS

Given that we have now accepted that sensations differ in kind from physical events, we now turn to examine the variety of proposals that have been put forward, both by philosophers and psychologists, as to the relationship that obtains between the two.

One suggestion, often put forward, is that sensations might be correlated with some specific neural activity, for example, the sensation of red may be correlated with the firing of neurons in the visual cortex. However, according to this view, although the two are correlated, it is supposed that sensations have no causal role in the production of behaviour (or indeed anything else). There are three versions of this idea.

1   Epiphenomenalism. Sensations are caused by the firing of neurons, but they themselves have no causal effects.
2   A sensation is a property of an otherwise material object or collection of objects. According to this opinion, a sensation is a property of some physical object or objects (e.g. a neuron or group of neurons), analogous to the properties of weight or size, but is not itself a physical property. As in the case of epiphenomenalism, the sensation has no causal role. If the reader finds it unclear what the difference is between a sensation being a property of a material object and an epiphenomenon, then she is in good company: we believe that the difference, if there is one, is unclear and inconsequential.
3   Parallelism. Sensations run in parallel with material events, events such as the firing of neurons, but are not caused by these events and have no effect upon them.

Psychologists who accept one of the three options described above are often inclined to leave it at that, saying something to the effect that that's OK; we are interested in behaviour, and since each of the three options implies that consciousness has no causal effects, any one of the three versions listed above implies that we can have a scientific study of both behaviour and the internal mechanisms that bring it about (neurons), without having to consider consciousness at all. Thus, they just put consciousness to one side and ignore it.

Now, this may be a defensible position for the 'working' psychologist to take, but with respect to the nature of the world generally, it is not satisfactory (to put it mildly, we think). Over the past 500 years, science has provided us with a generally coherent and integrated account of the physical world. Consciousness, for example, being in pain or having a sensation of red, seems to be quite distinct from what is postulated in that account. Moreover, there is no obvious puzzle about the world to which consciousness might be the key to solving – for example, filling some kind of gap (since there appears to be no gap). At best, all we seem to have is a seeming correlation between material events (neurons firing) and sensations – analogous merely to the list of connections between names and numbers in a telephone dictionary (and nothing else). Put another way, the world of the observable seems to be complete without the mental. Also, given that sensations play no causal role in behaviour, it is not clear why we should have them (they have no function from an evolutionary point of view), and therefore there is no plausible reason for them having been selected in evolution. More generally, why should we be aware of anything? Our own view is that the fact that we are unable to adequately address these other questions suggests that we still have some fundamental lack of understanding concerning consciousness.

In addition to the three possible relations between sensations and physical events that we have described above (each of which assumes that sensations have no causal role in the production of behaviour), there is also another possibility, called interactionism. According to advocates of this possibility (e.g. Elitzur, 2009), sensations and neurons interact, in that the activation of neurons may cause sensations and sensations may activate neurons. Thus, according to this hypothesis, the assumption we have been making up to the present time – that a complete description of the relation between environmental input and behaviour can be given solely in physical terms (as depicted in Figure 11.1) – is false. For the reasons given above (i.e. the world of the physical seems to be internally complete), interactionism is not often advocated by scientists (including psychologists). At the very least, psychologists generally prefer to get on with observing and formulating theories solely in terms of physical structure (as described in Chapters 6 and 7) in the hope that "It will all work out in the end."

With respect to interactionism, we will only point out that it is a testable hypothesis. For if no solely physical account is sufficient to explain some behaviour, then presumably there would be some physical laws which we can observe to be violated; for example, some neurons would behave differently to others, and their action would not be explicable in terms of more basic physics and chemistry. Note, however, that we would still have the oddity that, seemingly, we would have non-observable events interacting with physical events in the case of only one sort of event in the world (i.e. the occurrence of human and perhaps animal behaviour).

Final comment: We believe that we can draw the following conclusion: there is no general agreement concerning what consciousness is, or its role (if any) in the explanation of behaviour. With this conclusion in mind, we leave you with the following two opinions. Blackmore (2001, p. 525) suggests, with respect to consciousness, that

> one day psychologists will look back and laugh at the silly muddle we got ourselves into. To them the way out may be obvious. The trouble is that right now, like everyone else in the field, I cannot see it.

And, by contrast, McGinn (1991) has argued that the problem concerning the relation between sensations and physical events will forever remain insoluble: that we humans lack the capacity to solve it. And what do we, the authors of this book, think? Well, we have different views, which the interested reader may wish to read about (Harley, 2017; Wilton, 2016).

Test your understanding of Chapter 11

1   It is often claimed that human consciousness poses a problem for explanation in psychology. Explain, and discuss this claim.

2   "A mere echo, the faint rumour left behind by the disappearing 'soul' upon the air of philosophy" (William James, 1904, *Does Consciousness Exist?*). Discuss.

3   "Consciousness: the having of perceptions, thoughts and feelings; awareness. The term is impossible to define except in terms that are unintelligible without a grasp of what consciousness means. . . . Nothing worth reading has been written about it" (Sutherland, 1989, 'Consciousness', entry in the *International Dictionary of Psychology*). Discuss.

Summary of Part 2

Understanding behaviour

We do not have a conventional summary for this part (Part 2) of our book. For, unlike Part 1, we have not presented any general train of argument that can be summarised. However, the topics which have been discussed are related in that they address the variety of possible goals and levels of explanation sought in psychology. We have also examined other issues which arise in studying psychology, such as whether or not human beings have free will, the nature of intentional explanation, and the nature of consciousness. Questions pertaining to moral culpability, and crime and punishment, have also arisen. Consequently, rather than present a summary, we shall draw a conclusion. Our conclusion is that psychology can and should be a fascinating subject to study, not only in its technical aspects but also because it may open one's eyes to a variety of significant issues concerned with the way we humans see ourselves.

PART 3

What psychology tells us about the practice of science

In these two chapters, we consider the contribution that psychology has made to our understanding of scientific progress. Some contribution to an understanding could be expected given that progress of any sort, scientific or cultural, must depend upon the kind of beings that we humans are.

CHAPTER 12

The use of imagery in scientific thought

It will be recalled that in Chapters 1–5 of this book, we examined the structure of scientific explanation. We can think of those chapters as describing and providing an understanding of the constraints on an explanation in order for it to be called scientific. For example, a scientific explanation must be open to test by observation. Now let us consider a different but related issue. Suppose for any set of data, there are a number of logically possible different scientific theories (explanations) that could explain these data. It seems plausible to suppose that human beings may not readily be able to formulate some of these theories, and perhaps could not even formulate others at all. (By contrast, perhaps Martians whose 'brains' may differ fundamentally from ours might find it easy to formulate some of the theories we find difficult to formulate, and hard to formulate some of the theories we find easy to formulate; however, we shall be concerned only with human beings!)

A distinction can be made between two kinds of ways in which our thinking may be limited. One way in which it may be limited lies in the amount of information that can be processed. For example, although a person may be able to multiply 25 by 76 in their head, perhaps they would not be able to multiply 255 by 766 in similar fashion. They need more computing power. This limitation is, however, not the kind of limitation we are going to examine here. Rather, we shall consider a limitation in the ways (modes, methods) of thinking the brain can employ. What is meant by different ways of thinking should become apparent as we work through this chapter.

In this chapter, we shall consider work by psychologists that has given us some understanding of a particular limitation which we believe has greatly affected advances in the history of science. It will first be pointed out that in solving problems mentally, people often employ imagery – a method of problem solving that has distinctive characteristics. It will then be argued that not only is this method of solving problems used in science, it is the method we are disposed to use, even when a problem does not demand it. Perhaps, then, attempting to solve problems with the aid of imagery is the only method of solving problems that we are capable of employing effectively, and we are much less capable of using other methods.

We then turn to the history of science. If there are limitations in our ability to formulate scientific theories, one might expect (predict) that in the history of science, there has been a progression of theories from those most easily conceived to ones less easily conceived, with the latter supplanting the former only when the former have been shown to be inadequate. Therefore, since psychologists have discovered that we are disposed to use imagery in mental problem-solving, one could expect that the early theories would be ones that can be formulated by the use of imagery, and the later ones not so. It will be argued that this is indeed the case, and hence that evidence from experiments in psychology supports the claim that there are psychological constraints on our ability to engage in scientific theorising.

CHARACTERISTICS OF MENTAL PROBLEM-SOLVING

Human beings are able to solve mental problems by using a process that, in several respects, is *analogous to making relevant observations of physical objects in their environment*. The process is familiar to us all in that it consists of using imagery. Here is one example: suppose you are asked how many windows there are in your house. An obvious way of solving this problem is simply by making relevant observations, for example, by walking round your house, looking at the windows, and counting them. But suppose you are asked to solve the problem when you are not in the vicinity of your house. Typically, you would then solve it by imagining walking round the house, look-ing up at the windows, and counting them. One can call this the method of using imagery. In three clear-cut ways, the method is analogous to making relevant observations of the world. This can be seen most clearly with refer-ence to some classic experiments and illustrations in psychology.

Consider a classic experiment carried out by Shepard and Metzler (1971). Participants were shown two pictures, A and B, simultaneously. Picture A depicted a two-dimensional view of an arm-like object of several three-dimensional blocks fitted together. The other picture (B) depicted either the same object as viewed from a different angle or a different object (typically a mirror image of A). The participant's task was to respond "yes" or "no" as quickly as possible according to whether the same object was shown in the two pictures (see Figure 12.1).

The results of these experiments strongly suggest two of the ways in which solving the problem is analogous to making relevant observations in the world.

1   First the participants say that their experience in solving the problem is similar to the *experience* they would have if they were seeing the 'prob-lem' being solved by watching object A actually rotating to present the point of view from which object B would be observed.
2   To appreciate the second way in which solving the problem is similar to making observations in the world, consider what would occur if a person were to observe an actual rotation of A to bring it into a 'match' with B. Then, as the object rotates, it would, with each 'step' in the rotation, cause a representation (percept) of the object to be generated internally

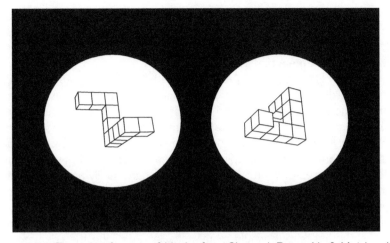

Figure 12.1 Example of a pair of blocks from Shepard, Roger N., & Metzler, Jacqueline. (1971). Mental rotation of three-dimensional objects. *Science, 171*(3972), 701–703. Reprinted with permission from AAAS.

as seen from the angle then displayed, until that percept matched the percept of B and the observer reports "yes" (a match). In such an experiment, the time taken to report the match would, obviously, increase as a linear (straight line) function of the number of steps taken in rotation for the two displays to match.

Now, bearing in mind that what we have just seen would occur if a person were to observe the rotation of A, consider what was shown by the results of the actual experiment (see Figure 12.1). The results showed that, on "yes" trials, reaction time (RT) was a linear function of the angle through which object A would have to rotate to yield the same view as object B. This result suggests that the internal process in solving the problem consists, in part, of a succession of internal states (images) that are similar to the internal states (percepts) that would be produced if one were to *perceive* the one object (A) rotating into the position of the other object (B).

Shepard called the process that operates in this experiment "mental rotation". Of course, nothing actually rotates in the problem-solver's head. Rather, a succession of internal states occurs that are analogous to (a simulation of) the internal states that would be induced if the subject were to perceive the object rotating.

A third respect in which problem solving may be analogous to perceiving can be described as follows. Suppose we ask a person the following question: if a cube measuring two inches along each side and coloured on one of its sides were to be divided into cubes measuring one inch on each side, how many sides of the resulting cubes would be coloured? The person is likely to report that they imagine the cube being cut up, just as they would perceive an actual cube being cut up. Moreover, if you ask them which particular face of the original cube was coloured, they will readily provide an answer (e.g. top), and often name a particular colour.

Now, why is the account given by the participant in this experiment, concerning the division of the cube, interesting? The fact that the person will readily name a particular face and perhaps a particular colour shows that in solving the problem, they manipulate information that is *logically irrelevant* to the solution. In order to work out the answer to the question "How many faces would be coloured?", it is not logically necessary to specify that some *particular* face is coloured or what that colour is. You can readily appreciate this by noting that the answer to the question would be the same, whichever face is coloured and whatever the colour. And, consistent with this, there are ways of solving the problem by not specifying these aspects of the cube. For example, using mathematics, one would merely, say, let side x be the coloured side, where x could be any side and any colour. Shepard called these unnecessary attributes *extra baggage* (e.g. see Shepard & Feng, 1972).

The manipulation of irrelevant information strongly suggests that participants solve the problem by simulating a perception of a cube being cut up. Physical objects necessarily have shape, extension, and colour. In perception, each of these aspects is normally (perhaps invariably) represented in the percept; for example, we don't see just the shape of an object and not its size. Similarly, in solving the cube problem, all aspects of the object tend to be represented, or at least more aspects than are necessary to solve the problem. Hence, it seems likely that the process of problem solving is a *simulation* of perception, rather than a separate process that has evolved entirely independently for problem solving. (Presumably, if it had evolved independently, it would not involve the manipulation of irrelevant information.)

The example of the cube being cut up illustrates extra baggage. But it does not, in itself, show that extra baggage may actually make the solving of a problem more difficult. So we shall now look at another example which shows that extra baggage can make solving a problem more difficult. Let's first remind ourselves of the game of noughts and crosses, illustrated on the right in Figure 12.2. There are two players (Mary and John) with nine vacant squares before them. Taking turns, each player selects one of the squares and places within it either an X (Mary) or a 0 (John). The aim of each player is to form as many straight lines of Xs (Mary) or 0s (John) as they can, with the winner being the one that forms the most.

Simon (1969, p. 76) invented a game, which he called number scrabble, the structure of which is isomorphic with (corresponds to) noughts and crosses. The two players are faced with a single pool of nine chips, face-upward, numbered 1–9. Taking turns, each player selects one of the chips, whilst retaining the ones they have already selected. The aim of each player is to form as many triads of chips that add up to 15 as they can. The winner is the one who has formed the most triads when all the chips have been taken from the pool. The isomorphism with noughts and crosses can be

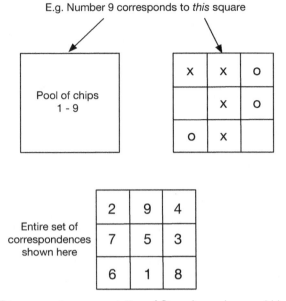

Figure 12.2 Diagrammatic representation of Simon's number scrabble.

seen by referring to the lower portion of Figure 12.2. By numbering the squares appropriately in the noughts and crosses game, it can be seen that any triad of chips that adds up to 15 (e.g. 2, 9, 4, or 2, 5, 8) corresponds to a possible row of Xs or Os.

You might ask why, in noughts and crosses, Mary (say) has Xs only and John has Os only, whereas in number scrabble there is no obvious differentiation. The answer is, of course, that in noughts and crosses, the differentiation is made to indicate which player has made a particular mark in the array, whereas in number scrabble each player has their own accumulated 'pile' of selected chips in front of them, indicating which chips are theirs.

We have seen that the two games are *isomorphic* – that is, they map onto each other. Nevertheless, as Simon (1969, p. 76) reports,

> Players who know how to play noughts and crosses are unable to carry their skill over to number scrabble and even when they learn of the correspondence are able to exploit it only by superimposing an internal representation of the number scrabble onto an internal (visual) representation of noughts and crosses – rather than being able to extract properties common to the two games, representing these properties internally and being able to use them.

When taking a class on this topic, one of the authors of this book used to tell the students that problem solvers who had learned to play both games could not form an abstract representation common to both. But when, in one meeting of the class, a student asked him what he meant by 'abstract', he could not answer the question. He should have said that players cannot form a single representation which encompasses the fact that the relation between the members of a point-scoring triad of numbers (i.e. they add up to 15) is the same as the relation between a point-scoring triad of the squares (as depicted in Figure 12.2). The use of the word 'abstract' by the lecturer was just a means, perhaps non-intentional, of avoiding having to think about what was shared by the tasks.

Thus, to repeat: the conclusion to be drawn from Simon's study is that persons cannot extract and use properties that are common to the two games. That is, they cannot form an internal representation of a game that would obtain at some higher level than that of the sensory input. They seem only to be able to use a process of imagining the various possible moves in the two perceptually distinct games. If they could extract the information common to the two games, there would be a transfer of skill from one game to the other, and therefore better performance. This example goes beyond the cube-cutting example in that it shows that there is an inability to extract only those aspects of the problem which are necessary for solving the problem, even when not extracting those aspects is inefficient.

ARE HUMANS DISPOSED TO USE IMAGERY IN SOLVING PROBLEMS?

It will be suggested here that people are *disposed* to use imagery in solving problems even when there is nothing in the problem that demands it. Similarly, they are disposed to use imagery in thinking and understanding. And, following the presentation of our case for such a disposition, we shall then go further by proposing that they may sometimes be constrained to solve problems by imagery, and therefore are unable to readily solve some problems when those problems are not amenable to solution by the use of imagery.

Before considering some examples that show persons are disposed to use imagery, it is important to realise that it only *makes sense* to ask whether a person is disposed to solve a problem in a particular way if there is a logically possible alternative way of solving it. In other words, it makes sense to say that persons are disposed to use imagery for solving a particular problem (or in thinking or understanding) only if it is logically possible that the problem could be solved by a different method (perhaps by a Martian, or the use of mathematics). Therefore, in the examples we will now describe of being disposed to using imagery, we shall show also that there is at least one alternative method of solving the problem.

EXAMPLES OF OUR DISPOSITION TO USE IMAGERY

Our first example is the simple cube-division problem described earlier. As was pointed out, this problem could be solved mathematically without including the extra baggage of specifying which face of the cube was coloured and the colour of that face. Yet people do not use this logically possible alternative way; rather, they use imagery.

Our second example comes from our own experience, and we believe would be shared by all those who have endeavoured to explain some concept to a class of students who are otherwise unfamiliar with that concept. For illustration, suppose a lecturer in experimental design is about to explain the concept of an interaction between independent variables (in their effect upon some dependent variable). The lecturer describes the concept *precisely*. That is, the lecturer states that an interaction between variables occurs when the effect of one of the variables depends upon the value of the other. Surely, the lecturer thinks, that's all there is to it – what could be simpler? But the students just look blankly at the lecturer – clearly, they have no idea what the lecturer is talking about! However, suppose now that the lecturer gives an example, one such as the following. Suppose one asks a doctor what, if any, is the effect of eating fatty foods on the probability of death by heart attack. The doctor responds by saying,

> Well, it all depends: it depends upon whether you are asking about males or females. In the cases of males, there is a large effect such that the more fat is eaten the shorter the life expectancy. On the other hand, in the case of females, the effect, although of the same kind, is a much smaller one.

In other words, the variable of amount of fat eaten interacts with gender: that is, the effect of the one variable (fatty food intake) depends upon the value of the other variable (gender). When an *example* such as this is presented, the faces of the audience light up in wreathes of smiles! (We exaggerate slightly.) And it's even better if the lecturer presents an accompanying diagram to illustrate the interaction.

This experience of providing examples to aid understanding is so common that one tends not to realise how peculiar it should seem. The original definition, given by the lecturer, without an example *exactly* specifies the form taken by any interaction. That is, it contains *all* the information required to specify what an interaction is. Almost certainly a computer endowed with artificial intelligence could readily follow the meaning of the words in the definition and apply that definition in any actual case. No additional information is needed.

Yet, giving an example works wonders upon human understanding, even though the example includes the 'extra baggage' (particularities) of an individual case, in the same way that the colour red is a particularity of some individual cube. Why is the example so helpful? The answer is that it assists comprehension by utilising the mechanism of solving problems by the use of imagery: giving an example 'clothes' the necessary components of the general case with the sensory attributes of an individual case – the only cases one ever encounters in perception.

Our third example concerns thinking in mathematics. In geometry, what constitutes an angle, a line, a point, or any other element is defined in terms of the relations between the elements. For example, a straight line is defined as the shortest distance between two points; parallel lines are defined as lines which never meet, no matter what their length. The system as a whole, constituted of all the elements, defined by their relations to each other, is called a syntactic system.

The syntactic system that we call geometry may have practical applications which involve an *interpretation* of the elements; so, for example, the element 'line', as defined within the system, may be taken to represent a line in physical space. The practical application of geometry involves manipulating the elements of the system to yield a deduction, with the results of the deduction having, in turn, a correspondence with the physical world of space. For example, from the basic definitions of the elements and their relations, one could deduce that the angles of any three-sided figure add up to 180 degrees.

Even though the geometry as a syntactic system is complete (each element is defined in relation to each other, and the process of deduction is well established), mathematicians find it helpful to construct diagrams on paper in order to solve geometrical problems, and failing that, to imagine diagrams (see Hadamard, 1945, pp. 75–99). Those of you who have studied geometry will appreciate how the drawing of diagrams can assist one's thinking.

However, helpful though the drawing of diagrams as an aid to thinking may be, it is not only unnecessary, it can actually be misleading. It can be misleading because it surreptitiously suggests that there is only one sort of geometry – that which can be represented in diagrams on paper. (It is called Euclidean geometry.) In fact, there are a variety of different geometries, each with different relations specifying the elements; and not all can be represented by drawings or models in two- or three-dimensional space. This fact was realised only in the 19th century, even though scholars and practical men (they were all men at that time) had been familiar with (Euclidean) geometry both as a means of abstract thinking and application since about 300 BC. So again, we see limitations in our capacity for thought, inasmuch as an interpretation of the syntax in terms of perceived or imagined spatial layouts has the effect of inhibiting thinking about the possibility of syntactical systems which cannot be so interpreted.

CONCLUSIONS SO FAR

1   Human beings use imagery to solve problems. Moreover, they are *disposed* to use imagery even when the problem is not cast in such a form as to suggest that it is this process that should be used. This finding suggests that people lack well-developed mechanisms for solving problems by other means.

2   Insofar as the use of imagery solves problems in a specialised way (as indicated by the characteristics of imagery and its relation to perception), there may be problems which are not amenable to solution by this

method. There may be problems which cannot be cast in the form of concrete objects requiring manipulation in space and time. Hence, there may be some problems that are soluble in principle, but in fact cannot readily be solved by the human mind because the mind lacks a well-developed capability for using methods other than that of imagery.

THE HISTORY OF SCIENTIFIC THOUGHT

What follows is an analysis which we think would be hard to dispute. In the history of science, one might expect a progression to be apparent from theories which are easily conceived to ones which are less easily conceived, with the latter presumably being thought of only when the former fail to yield correct predictions. Hence, for us humans, one might expect a progression in scientific theories from those that refer to entities which have the sensory characteristics of perception (even though such entities may only be imagined) to more abstract entities which do not have sensory characteristics and therefore cannot be imagined – reflecting thereby an increase in difficulty of conception.

Consider the history of mechanics (see Butterfield, 1957, Chapter 1). According to Aristotle, a philosopher and scientist living in ancient Greece, the natural (normal) state of an object is to be at rest. An object moves only when a force is being applied to it. Remove the force and the object stops moving. Obviously, this claim is merely a simple extrapolation from what one ordinarily observes in the world. For example, when the horse that pulls a cart comes to a halt, the cart stops moving. The Aristotelians realised, of course, that there are exceptions to this effect – for example, when an arrow leaves a bow, it continues moving even when the string no longer pushes it. But given the basic claim that an object moves only when a force is being applied to it, such obvious exceptions can perhaps be explained by ad hoc means – for example, the hypothesis that upon release of an arrow from a bow, the air rushes from the front of the arrow round to its back and pushes it forward (see Butterfield, 1957, Chapter 1).

Now consider the work of Newton, a scientist who lived in the 17th century. As we have seen in earlier chapters, according to Newton, an object remains in its state of *uniform motion or rest* unless acted upon by some external force. Now, the continued uniform motion of an object, with no force any longer acting upon it, is something we never actually observe; for example, even when a puck continues to move across the ice after being struck by the hockey stick, it eventually comes to rest because of the force generated by the friction between the puck and the ice. But what Newton did, in formulating his law, was to think of idealised objects (e.g. perfect spheres) in the idealised situation of completely empty space, so that he could consider them removed from the various forces (e.g. friction or gravitation) that actually affect them in any real situation. He then applied the principles derived from these thought experiments to real cases. Hence, there is a degree of abstraction in thought not found in Aristotle. However, note that Newton is still thinking by reference to objects and space, the stuff of the perceived world. His thinking is very much based upon what he has actually seen, although it involves an extrapolation to what cannot be seen – rather like imagining a unicorn, consisting of familiar parts in an unfamiliar arrangement which, as far as we know, does not actually exist.

It is of interest also to consider the work of Kekulé (in the 19th century), since it clearly reveals the use of imagery in solving a problem, complete with 'extra baggage' (see McKellar, 1957; Shepard, 1978). Kekulé was interested in the structure of the benzene molecule, which at that time was unknown. For some time, he had been trying to work out how the various atoms that constitute the molecule are linked (connected) to each other. Then, when sitting by the fire in a dream-like state, he 'saw' in his imagination a number of snakes hooked together, each one biting the tail of the other. This ring-like structure gave him the essential point: that the molecule consisted of a ring of atoms hooked together. This discovery was a great advance in knowledge since the molecular structure of all the other substances which had been examined before then had been one of linear chains of connected atoms.

More generally, prior to the 20th century one can see in physics and chemistry a degree of abstraction in solving problems as compared to the Aristotelian reliance upon actual perception. However, creative thinking is still 'concrete' in that the theories then being proposed postulate the sorts of entities familiar in daily perception. For example, in addition to the cases described above, kinetic theory postulates a large number of very small elastic billiard ball-like particles. The structure of light is supposedly either like the waves on a pond (Huygens) or particles (Newton). Atomic theory postulates a miniature solar system. Furthermore, as described earlier, Euclidian geometry, which maps onto our three-dimensional perception of the world, is the only geometry available to represent the structure of space. The uniformity in the sorts of things postulated (i.e. entities which can readily be imagined) is striking.

Thus, we see that prior to the 20th century, the practice of science (theory construction) was limited by the capacity to conceive most readily the sorts of entities that can be imagined. In other words, the practice was limited to that of taking a concrete case and postulating some imagined entity that is analogous to it.

Now, by contrast with all the cases described above, consider 20th-century science. Twentieth-century science saw the advent of relativity theory and quantum mechanics. The general theory of relativity postulates four dimensions of space-time which are far removed from our perceptual experience of three spatial dimensions and one of time, and in doing so uses a non-Euclidean geometry to represent space. Euclidean geometry is the geometry which you learned at school – a geometry in which, for example, the sum of the angles of a triangle equals 180 degrees. In a non-Euclidean geometry, this may not be so. Try to imagine such a triangle – you cannot do it. Quantum mechanics strikes one as very peculiar (see Feynman,

1967, Chapter 6). The reason for this is that it uses terms in its equations which have no direct interpretation with respect to the structure of matter as we ordinarily perceive it. For example, one cannot map the terms onto either waves or particles. The terms in the equations work to predict various observable effects, with no failures of prediction and without contradiction; but individually they have no concrete interpretation. So now we have a theory which is abstract in the extreme. Indeed, Feynman is thought to have said something along the lines of, "If you think you understand it, you don't understand it", by which he meant that there can be no understanding of it other than being able to manipulate the equations in order to deduce observable consequences.

In summary, the claim made here has been that the progression in science from the concrete to the abstract is no accident. Science begins with the formulation of the most easily conceived theories (easily conceived for the human mind/mechanism) and moves to less easily conceived theories only when the easy theories fail. And, for humans, the theories most easily conceived are the ones that employ our well-developed problem-solving mechanism of imagery.

1   Describe the contribution that cognitive psychology has made to our understanding of the historical progression of scientific theories.
2   Speaking of Java man, Quine (1953) wrote:
     The unrefined and sluggish mind
     Of Homo Javanensis
     Could only think of things concrete
     And open to the senses.
     To what extent has psychology shown this to be true also of *Homo sapiens*?

Test your understanding of Chapter 12

CHAPTER 13

Why are cultures that practice science better at controlling the material world than non-scientific cultures?

In both scientific and non-scientific cultures, attempts are made to control and predict the behaviour of other persons and the environment. Yet in cultures in which science is practiced, prediction and control have been more successful than in cultures in which science is or was not practiced. Modern Western society is the obvious case in which science is practiced, and for which it can be argued that economic changes since the 16th century are largely dependent upon the advance of science and its technological application, as illustrated by the electric light, dentistry, television, the motor car, and many other possible examples. In Western society, we have seen a rapid advance in control that is unique in the history of mankind, over several thousand years and over all cultures. So what is it about science, or the environment in which science is practiced, that accounts for this control? Relevant studies in history, sociology, and psychology suggest some possible answers. In this chapter, we shall consider a number of possible answers, not necessarily mutually exclusive. Each of them seems to us to be a plausible candidate, although you might well reject one or more of them and/or think of others that are equally plausible.

(A) STRUCTURE OF SCIENTIFIC THEORIES

One obvious thought is that there may be some important structural difference between explanations we call scientific and those we call non-scientific – some difference that accounts for the success of the former in their practical application. We examined what these differences are in Part 1 of this book. Taking our cue from what was said there, it might seem, at first sight, that the most obvious difference between scientific and non-scientific explanations is that a scientific explanation must be *open to test*, whereas a non-scientific one may not be. We say this since testability seems to be the criterion for an explanation to be scientific, and would seem to generate advances in understanding as various explanations are put aside when particular predictions fail to be confirmed. However, contrary to this suggestion, scientific and non-scientific explanations do not always differ in this respect. Horton (1967) examined non-scientific cultures which have (or had) little exposure to (interaction with) Western society. Suppose a 'medicine man' (they are usually men) is trying to predict whether a sick person will live or die (see Horton, 1971, p. 247). He may go through some elaborate procedure, akin to reading tea leaves, and thereby predict the death or recovery of the person. And he might attempt to manipulate events, predicting that if he casts a particular spell, this will cause the person to get well. Sometimes his prediction is confirmed, sometimes it is falsified. So, although the prediction is not tested in order to evaluate the truth of some law or theory, it is tested in its practical application: the patient either dies or recovers. Another example would be one in which a person (for simplicity, call him a medicine man also) performs a rain dance in drought, with the prediction that this will produce rain. Sometimes the prediction is confirmed, sometimes it is falsified: either it rains or it doesn't. It seems clear, therefore, that in the non-scientific culture, some explanations are testable in that predictions are made, and these sometimes fail. So, on grounds of testability, there seems to be no qualitative difference between the two sorts of account. Thus, this obvious candidate for accounting for the differential success of cultures which practice science seems to be ruled out.

However, you might suggest that there may be another qualitative difference between the two types of explanation. This is that accounts such as the one given by the medicine man can always be saved by adjustment, whereas scientific ones cannot. With respect to some of the practices of the medicine man, Horton (1967, p. 171) says "Nearly all the procedures are thought to be very delicate and easily thrown out of kilter." For example, perhaps the chicken bones were not thrown into the air in quite the right way or the sun was overcast by a cloud. There are many built-in possibilities for the wrong prediction being made, whilst still preserving the basic integrity of the procedure (and the reputation of the practitioner). But is it true that scientific accounts cannot be preserved when they make a prediction that fails? No, for as we have seen in Part 1 of this book, explanations in science can also be saved regardless of some seeming refutation. Recall, for example, that given the result of the Michelson and Morley experiment, the theory that light travels through the ether (space) at a constant speed could be saved by changing an auxiliary assumption concerning the instruments used to measure distance (a change to one of assuming that a measuring rod shortens in the direction parallel to the direction of the movement of the rod). In both cultures, scientific and non-scientific, any single belief is interconnected with all other beliefs, forming a web of beliefs, and any one belief may be saved by changing one or more of the other beliefs (Hesse, 1974). Thus, in both cultures, scientific and non-scientific, the failure to make a correct prediction can be attributed to some variable which may leave the essence of some theory or practice untouched; the logic is the same.

Perhaps, however, there may be another difference (and this time perhaps a real one) between scientific and non-scientific accounts. This is that scientific theories must be internally consistent and economical in explanation, for it is these characteristics that permit good prediction and control. Indeed, as we saw in Chapter 5, in the extreme case of complexity within a theory, there is no prediction or control. Perhaps procedures practiced in a non-scientific culture are not subject to such constraints and there is no social pressure to insist that they do. Hence the medicine man, in adjusting his account, can 'get away with anything'. We leave unresolved the question of whether there is this difference.

Overall it seems to us that the differential control of the material world in different societies seems not to be a result of scientific explanations being different in logical structure from the explanations put forward in non-scientific cultures. This means that we should look elsewhere for the relevant factor or factors.

So, let's now consider a number of possibilities other than testability which might plausibly be a determinant of the practical success of science. Bear in mind that, as stated earlier, these are not always mutually exclusive, and there may be other possibilities of which we may be unaware.

(B) THE DEVELOPMENT OF THE WRITTEN WORD

The advance of 'knowledge' in any domain is probably aided if a person's thoughts and ideas are written down (see MacCulloch, 2003). Any contradictions within that person's thought may then become apparent, for example, ones that arise in saying one thing one day and a contradictory thing on another day. Furthermore, mass copies of written material, first made possible by Gutenberg around 1440, enabled the written word to be disseminated to many more people, each of whom could have been stimulated to further thought, and, more generally, constituted a type of cultural memory. These advantages apply at least as much to thinking in science as in other domains. Note also that, being invented in the 15th century, the printing press became available at about the same time as science began to take off, just as one might expect if it were indeed a catalyst for scientific advance. It should also be noted, however, that this period, called the Reformation, was also the occasion for other changes that might have been helpful. We discuss some of these below.

(C) THE SYSTEMATIC TESTING OF IDEAS

As stated above, ideas about how the world works are often tested, not only in scientific cultures but also in non-scientific cultures, by virtue of practical applications either being successful or failing. Indeed, it could hardly be otherwise if we are using our so-called knowledge to control the world: the act of attempting to control the world is, implicitly, a testing of the idea. However, it seems to us that merely discovering one's predictions to be false (say, the prediction that drug X will be followed by the recovery of a patient), with subsequent attempts to explain the failure, may differ in important ways from the testing of ideas carried out in science. In science, one attempts to test one's ideas *systematically*. In the systematic testing of the effect of a variable X (the independent variable) upon another variable Y (the dependent variable), *one compares the effect of X with that of not-X* (i.e. value of X = 0).

If the difference between the two sorts of testing is important, it may be argued that scientific advance has much to do with the application of the rather (humdrum) experimental method of systematic test, as contrasted with the testing that is implicit in the predictions made by non-scientists. Moreover, if the systematic testing of one's ideas is, in some sense, an unnatural practice (as we shall shortly show the evidence suggests), this could explain why not all cultures have adopted it, for we should not then expect that it would normally be adopted merely as a consequence of human beings having considerable intelligence. (We say this, even though you may think that it is obvious that one should engage in systematic testing. But perhaps that is because the reason for doing so was explained to you. We ask you to wait until we have made our case before you pass judgement.)

In order to see clearly the difference between systematic testing by the scientist and testing by the medicine man (say), let's consider a case in detail. Then, after that, we shall try to justify the claim that the former is an unnatural practice.

Let us consider first the systematic testing by the scientist, taking as an example what the standard experimental method would entail in the case of testing the hypothesis that, in times of drought, dancing produces rain. Over a period during which there were a number of droughts, we would randomly choose to dance during some of the droughts and on other randomly chosen occasions choose not to dance. Then we would compare the frequency with which rain follows each. Two alternative outcomes would be:

1   Rain follows dancing and non-dancing equally often (e.g. all the time; some of the time; none of the time). Hence, we could conclude that dancing probably does not cause it to rain.
2   Rain follows dancing more frequently than no dancing. Hence, we could conclude that dancing probably does cause it to rain.

Of course, we might also carry out a statistical analysis to demonstrate this conclusion more formally, but such an analysis is a procedural sophistication that we need not consider here. Similarly, we might consider the possibility that confounded variables are at work, but again we need not consider this. The critical aspect of the procedure is that a *comparison* is made between dancing and no dancing.

Now consider what the medicine man does. Since the aim of dancing is to produce rain, we presume that the medicine man *only and always* dances when drought occurs. Given this, let's consider the possible outcomes.

1   Suppose it always rains after the medicine man dances. The medicine man argues that the dancing causes the rain. Neither he nor anyone else *compares* the consequences of dancing with no dancing. Hence, he fails to determine whether dancing has any effect (although he may

keep his job because he and others believe that the dancing produced the rain). Perhaps, for example, the medicine man always dances when it is three weeks into the drought (perhaps only then is the drought obvious), and it so happens that the climate is such that rain always follows a drought of three weeks.

2   Suppose it sometimes rains. The medicine man argues that the dancing ordinarily causes rain; but, sometimes something else interferes to prevent rain (or it rains only when additional conditions obtain). Again, neither he nor anyone else *compares* the frequency of rain following dancing with that following no dancing. Hence, he fails to determine whether dancing has any effect (although he may keep his job because he and others may believe that the dancing sometimes produces rain).

3   Suppose it never rains. Then the medicine man and others are unlikely to believe that dancing produces rain.

So, in conclusion, because no comparisons are systematically made, the medicine man may come to believe that dancing causes rain when it does not. More generally, he reasons as follows: if X occurs and X is followed by Y, then X causes Y. A scientist would not make this error since he or she would compare the consequences of dancing on some occasions when there is a drought with no dancing on other occasions when there is a drought.

Now let's turn to our claim that what the medicine man (and others in a non-scientific culture) are doing is learning about the world by the natural method used by animals and humans, and that, by contrast, the systematic testing of one's ideas is *an unnatural practice* (a breakthrough by the rational mind) which in part defines what it is to do science. This implies, of course, that science may not often feature in human society and makes it unsurprising that the development of science which has occurred over the last 500 years is unique in human history.

In order to appreciate what we mean by an unnatural practice, consider the following account of the *natural* way in which animals (including, as we shall see, human beings) learn about the world. Suppose a hungry pigeon is placed in a Skinner box which contains an illuminated disc on the wall, a disc which, if it is pecked, delivers food in the food hopper. Sooner or later the bird, by chance, pecks at the disc, and having done so eats the food then delivered. The pecking response is thus reinforced, and from then on the bird pecks the disc at a steady rate until satiated.

Now, in the simple experiment just described, the pecking of the disc caused the food to be delivered; and without thinking about it, we might assume that the law of reinforcement could be stated as follows. Whenever the emission of some behaviour causes the delivery of a reinforcer, such as food, the behaviour then increases in its frequency. However, this is not the correct statement of the law. As stated correctly, the law is that whenever the emission of some behaviour is *followed by* the delivery of a reinforcer, such as food, then the behaviour increases in its frequency. It is not necessary that the behaviour has to cause the food to be delivered in order for learning to occur.

Let's consider a classic demonstration of learning which highlights the distinction between 'causes food' and 'is followed by food'. Suppose we place a pigeon in a Skinner box in which food is delivered at intervals, regardless of the bird's behaviour. For example, perhaps the interval between deliveries varies randomly, about some mean, say one minute. What do we observe? Suppose that at the moment when the first delivery of food is made, the bird has just emitted some random (presumably) behaviour such as lifting its right leg. What we then observe is that the frequency of this behaviour (lifting the right leg) increases: the behaviour has been reinforced by virtue of having been *followed* by the food. And since the emission of the behaviour increases in frequency, the bird is more likely to be emitting this same behaviour than if it had not been reinforced. Therefore, it will be this behaviour that is more likely to be occurring when the next (random) delivery occurs – and so on for future deliveries, with the behaviour becoming more and more likely to be emitted just before a delivery occurs, until eventually the bird is engaged in lifting its leg continually. Skinner (1947) called such behaviour "superstitious behaviour". One might say that the animal believes that lifting its leg brings about the food.

Perhaps we should note that in our description of how superstitious behaviour comes about, we have simplified the process somewhat, but not in any way that is misleading with respect to what we wish to argue about systematic testing. Readers may consult Skinner's classic (1947) paper for more detail.

What we have described is, of course, consistent with classical (stimulus-response) associationism (as described in Chapter 2); and one can appreciate that in its natural environment, the pigeon, or any other animal, may, in behaving in the way we have described, learn enough about the world in order for it to survive. For example, it may learn that if it behaves in a particular way (B_1) in Situation X, it gets food. And it may also learn that if it behaves in the same way (B_1) in Situation Y, it does not get food, since although the response initially generalises to situation Y, it then extinguishes in that situation, as food never follows it. So, in due course, the bird emits only behaviours that are followed by food, and to that extent is behaving efficiently.

However, note that the pigeon does not find out whether it is the doing of B_1 in Situation X that causes the food to 'be delivered': *perhaps the food would be available anyway without the occurrence of B_1*. The case is analogous to that of the medicine man described previously in this chapter. Such learning about the world is inefficient as compared with the method of systematic testing. What the bird 'should' do, in Situation X, is compare the consequences of behaving with the consequences of not behaving. What it actually does (repeat any behaviour that is followed by food) is the *natural* method for behaving adaptively, but not the best method.

This most natural method is used not only by pigeons and persons in those societies which some might consider to be primitive. Consider the following example. A young athlete injures a muscle in their leg. The athlete then sees a physiotherapist for treatment (possibly one that has been recommended by others). The therapist says that a particular form of massage will heal the tissue, and, accordingly, provides massage twice a week. Within a month, the leg is back to normal and the treatment is deemed to have been a great success. Both physiotherapist and patient may believe that it has been a success. Furthermore, the physiotherapist has a number of letters from previous patients expressing their gratitude for a similar treatment given to them on previous occasions.

Now, any psychology student will know that in order to assess whether the treatment did indeed have a beneficial effect, one needs to compare the giving of the treatment with a control condition in which no treatment is given. Only by this means can the effectiveness or otherwise of the treatment be determined. (The tissues might well have healed over time, regardless of the treatment given.) But the physiotherapist, the patient, and the patients who wrote letters of thanks have not had the benefit of all this being explained to them – so, in essence, they use the rule "If X is followed by Y, then X causes Y".

The difference between the student and the non-student is not one of intellect: clever, educated persons can make the same mistake. By virtue of innate disposition, they, like Skinner's pigeon, do not readily think of such an unnatural practice! The idea of carrying out a systematic test, focusing on a comparison of conditions, is not something that is inherently within our intellectual repertoire. It is an unnatural practice. It has to be taught, and is absent in non-scientific cultures.

One may, incidentally, ask why the method of testing has not, over time, evolved as a natural disposition in the various species (including human beings). The answer might be that ordinarily in the natural environment, an animal has insufficient resources of energy to engage in testing – food may be so scarce that they have to spend all their time seeking it. Hence, even if in reproduction there were some mutation that disposed an animal to engage in testing, the animal would starve when testing the efficacy of some behaviour that seems to yield food (perhaps even if the behaviour were actually effective). Thus, the disposition to test, although innate in this animal, would fail to be passed on to the next generation. A student put forward this suggestion in one of our classes.

(D) DIFFERENT *A PRIORI* ASSUMPTIONS ABOUT THE WORLD

Perhaps people who live within in a non-scientific culture have fundamentally different assumptions about the world than those who live within a scientific culture. In a non-scientific culture, there is no attempt to discover what laws govern the world, because that culture does not have the belief that there are such laws (i.e. laws which would enable one to exercise control of the world). Perhaps in such a culture, all events outside the immediate control of man are to be explained by reference to the goals of some supernatural agent, with that agent not necessarily behaving in a lawful manner. So, for example, in the Middle Ages (approximately 400–1500 AD), the winning of some particular battle may have been credited to an act of God, and an earthquake may have been interpreted as a punishment for offending the Gods in some way. And a prophet may have made some prediction, believing that God intended to bring about some particular event in the world, but would not necessarily assume that God would act in the same way on other similar occasions. Thus, in general, persons in these cultures may have lacked the motivation to try to understand the world in terms of what rules (laws) hold sway – because they did not have the belief that there are such laws to be discovered (see Easton, 1961, p. 286; Frazer, 1922). Such a lack of belief that there are laws of nature may be contrasted with Newton's belief (about 1680) that the universe works like clockwork, an idea which could be said to have initiated the scientific revolution in the West (even though Newton believed that the mechanism was set up by God).

To modern readers, it may seem difficult to appreciate that human beings could, in the Middle Ages, readily believe in such capricious supernatural acts as we have described. However, one can ask whether their beliefs were any the less a result of considered thought than many of our beliefs. Consider, for comparison, the many minor events that would have occurred every day in the Middle Ages, each of which could readily be classified as acts of providence (acts of God) – for example, happening to find a place in a busy market where one can park one's cart. Now compare this with a modern analogue, such as being late for a meeting and finding that a nearby parking place, which on all previous occasions has already been taken, happens now to be free. Most of us would characterise such good fortune as a lucky coincidence, without any real thought as to what is meant by the expression 'a lucky coincidence', or whether the use of such an expression can be substantiated. (And, even now, in modern times, some people believe that the finding of a car parking space might be attributable to non-mechanistic forces, such as pure will – see Byrne, 2006.) Similarly, suppose one goes on holiday in Devon, finds oneself in a pub, and, surprise, surprise, sees an old friend with whom one has not communicated for 20 years sitting at the next table. This happened to one of us and was classified as a happy coincidence, and (more or less) thought about no more. Consider how many events like these are experienced in daily life; they are very common, and, as a matter of course, we tend to classify them as mere coincidences, thereby allowing us to pass over any serious thought as to their causes. In the Middle Ages, we suggest, they would have been explained by reference to providence – an act of God. Is such an explanation any the less considered or thoughtful?

(E) ACCEPTANCE OF FUNDAMENTAL CHANGE

Western societies typically are liberal in the sense that they tolerate free thought and therefore the emergence of alternative points of view. They are what Popper (1945) called "*open*" societies. By contrast, in "closed" societies (for example, the Middle Ages in Europe – see below), thought is restricted to views that are consistent with only a very limited set of possibilities. Thus, only one explanatory set of beliefs may be available to account for any event. Therefore, failures to make correct predictions are explained by ad hoc procedures within that limited set of beliefs. It is very unlikely that some radical alternative could be entertained.

We believe there is considerable merit in the idea, and that the development of an 'open society' accounts, in part, for the advance of science. In Western society, one set of beliefs can be more readily overturned by a very different set. It may be no accident that science 'took off' in the hundred years following the questioning of papal authority by Luther in Germany (16th century) and, separately, by King Henry the 8th in England (also 16th century). Such questioning, perhaps inevitably, led to the setting up of a number of opposing authorities which, in turn, led to *doubt* concerning where true authority lay. And this had the effect of forcing, and indeed encouraging, in the case of Luther, each person to decide for his or her self where the truth concerning different opinions of Christianity and its practice lay. The erosion of confidence in the power of authority to know the truth may have led also to a seeking of truth by means of considering evidence from the senses (the empirical approach of science), and reasoning – as opposed to having 'blind' faith in any authority, either religious (God) or secular (King).

A possible objection to the claim that new ideas are open to acceptance is that many individuals in an open society (e.g. psychoanalysts) seem unprepared to relinquish beliefs when these are seen to require many ad hoc adjustments in the face of evidence and argument. However, provided that some people (e.g. the young?) are ready to take up new ideas, with some being seen to be more successful in application than any prevailing opinion, a snowball effect may result. So the claim stands, regardless of the objection.

CONCLUSION

There may be a number of ways in which scientific and non-scientific cultures differ. These may concern basic beliefs about the world, the rational testing of ideas about how the world works, and the openness of society. Other factors, such as the printing press, may also be important.

---

1   Societies in which science is practiced have much greater control over the material world than societies in which science is not practiced. What might account for this?

2   Explain how it could be argued that the systematic testing of the effects of variables in science largely accounts for the success of science. Do you think the argument is plausible?

Test your understanding of Chapter 13

Summary of Part 3

Psychological constraints on scientific explanations

The two chapters of Part 3 have shown that the study of psychology may yield a greater understanding of the historical progression of scientific theories. And perhaps they have also provided a partial answer to the question of why the practice of science, although greatly effective in the practical control of nature for human benefit, has occurred only once in the history of humanity.

References

Atkins, P. (2004). Forward. In J. Baggott (Ed.), *Beyond measure: Modern physics, philosophy, and the meaning of quantum theory* (pp. xiii–xiv). Oxford: Oxford University Press.

Ayer, A.J. (1980). *Hume.* Oxford: Oxford University Press.

Bechtel, W. (1988). *Philosophy of science: An overview for cognitive science.* Hillsdale, NJ: Laurence Erlbaum Associates.

Blackmore, S. (2001). State of the art: The psychology of consciousness. *The Psychologist, 14,* 522–525.

Brentano, F. (1874). *Psychology from an empirical standpoint* (trans. A.C. Rancurello, D.B. Terrell, and L. McAlister). London: Routledge (1973).

Butler, S. (1872). *Erewhon: or, over the range.* London: Trubner & Co.

Butterfield, H. (1957). *The origins of modern science.* London: Bell & Sons.

Byrne, R. (2006). *The secret.* New York: Atria.

Campbell, C.A. (1951). Is 'free-will' a pseudoproblem? *Mind, 240,* 446–465.

Chomsky, N. (1965). *Aspects of the theory of syntax.* Cambridge, MA: MIT Press.

Conant, J.B. (1951). *Science and common sense.* New Haven: Yale University Press.

Dalrymple, B.T. (1994). *The age of the earth.* Stanford: Stanford University Press.

Darwin, C. (1859). *On the origin of species by natural selection.* London: John Murray.

Dennett, D.C. (1987). *The intentional stance.* Cambridge, MA: MIT Press/A Bradford Book.

Deutsch, J.A., & Clarkson, J.K. (1959). Reasoning in the hooded rat. *Quarterly Journal of Experimental Psychology, 11,* 150–154.

Donkin, C., & Nosofsky, R.M. (2012). The structure of short-term memory scanning: An investigation using response time distribution models. *Psychonomic Bulletin and Review, 19,* 363–394.

Duhem, P. (1954). *The aim and structure of physical theory.* Princeton, NJ: Princeton University Press (Originally published 1904).

Dunbar, R. (2004). *The human story: A new history of mankind's evolution.* London: Faber and Faber Ltd.

Easton, S.C. (1961). *The Western heritage: From the earliest times to the present day.* New York: Holt, Rinehart & Winston.

Elitzur, A.C. (2009). Consciousness makes a difference: A reluctant dualist's confession. In A. Batthyany & A.C. Elitzur (Eds.), *Irreducibly conscious: Alternatives to reductionist accounts of mind* (pp. 43–72). Heidelberg: Universitätsverlag Winter.

Elman, J.L. (Ed.). (1998). *Rethinking innateness: A connectionist perspective on development.* Cambridge, MA: MIT Press.

Eysenck, M., & Keane, M.T. (2015). *Cognitive psychology: A student's handbook* (6th ed.). Hove: Psychology Press.

Farah, M.J. (2010). *Neuroethics*. Cambridge, MA: MIT Press.

Feynman, R. (1967). *The character of physical law*. London: MIT Press.

FitzGerald, G.F. (1889). The ether and the earth's atmosphere, *Science, 13*, 390.

Fodor, J.A. (1975). *The language of thought*. New York: Thomas Y. Crowell.

Fodor, J.A. (1983). *The modularity of mind*. Cambridge, MA: MIT Press.

Frank, P. (1957). *Philosophy of science: The link between science and philosophy*. Mineola, NY: Dover Publications.

Frazer, J.G. (1922). *The golden bough: A study in comparative religion*. New York: Macmillan.

Freud, S. (1917). *Introductory lectures on psychoanalysis*. English edition Penguin Freud Library. Harmondsworth: Penguin (1991).

Gillies, D. (1993). *Philosophy of science in the twentieth century*. Oxford: Blackwell.

Greene, J., & Cohen, J. (2004). For the law, neuroscience changes nothing and everything. *Philosophical Transactions of the Royal Society of London, B: Biological Sciences, 359*, 1775–1785.

Gross, C.G. (1992). Representation of visual stimuli in inferior temporal cortex. *Philosophical Transactions of the Royal Society of London, B, 335*, 3–10.

Grunbaum, A. (2007). Is simplicity evidence of truth? *Royal Institute of Philosophy Supplement, 61*, 261–275.

Hadamard, J. (1945). *The mathematician's mind: The psychology of invention in the mathematical field*. Princeton, NJ: Princeton University Press.

Hall, C.S., Lindzey, G., & Campbell, J.B. (1997). *Theories of personality* (4th ed.). New York: John Wiley & Sons.

Harley, T.A. (2014). *The psychology of language* (4th ed.). Hove: Psychology Press.

Harley, T.A. (2017). *The science of consciousness*. Cambridge, MA: Cambridge University Press.

Hart, H.L.A. (1961). Legal responsibility and excuses. In S. Hook (Ed.), *Determinism and freedom* (pp. 95–116). London: Collier-MacMillan Ltd.

Hebb, D. (1949). *The organization of behavior*. New York: Wiley & Sons.

Hempel, C.G. (1958). Some reflection on the case for determinism. In S. Hook (Ed.), *Determinism and freedom* (pp. 170–175). New York: New York University Press.

Hempel, C.G. (1966). *Philosophy of natural science*. Englewood Cliffs, NJ: Prentice Hall.

Hesse, M. (1974). *The structure of scientific inference*. London: Macmillan.

Horton, R. (1967). African traditional thought and western science. *Africa, 37*, 50–71, 155–187.

Hospers, J. (1997). *An introduction to philosophical analysis* (4th ed.). London: Routledge & Keegan Paul.

Hull, C.L. (1943). *Principles of behavior: An introduction to behavior theory*. New York: Appleton-Century Company, Inc.

Hume, D. (1739). *A treatise of human nature* (ed. D.F. Norton and M.J. Norton). Oxford/New York: Oxford University Press (2000).

Jackson, F. (1982). Epiphenomenal qualia. *Philosophical Quarterly, 32*, 127–136.

James, W. (1904). Does 'consciousness' exist? *Journal of Philosophy, Psychology, and Scientific Methods, 1*, 477–491.

Kosslyn, S.M. (1973). Scanning visual images: Some structural implications. *Perception and Psychophysics, 14*, 90–94.

Kosslyn, S.M. (1994). *Image and brain: The resolution of the imagery debate*. Cambridge, MA: MIT Press.

Lakatos, I. (1978). *The methodology of scientific research programmes: Philosophical papers* (Vol. 1). Cambridge: Cambridge University Press.

Lashley, K.S. (1929). *Brain mechanisms and intelligence*. Chicago: University of Chicago Press.

Lashley, K.S. (1950). In search of the engram. *Society of Experimental Biology Symposium, 4*, 454–482.

Lewis, J.E. (2003). *The new rights of man*. London: Constable & Robinson.

Lorentz, H.A. (1892). The relative motion of the earth and the aether. *Zittingsverlag Akad. V. Wet, 1*, 74–79.

MacCulloch, D. (2003). *Reformation: Europe's house divided 1490–1700*. Harmondsworth: Penguin Books.

McGinn, C. (1991). *The problem of consciousness*. Oxford: Blackwell.

McKellar, P. (1957). *Imagination and thinking: A psychological analysis*. New York: Basic Books.

Michelson, A.A., & Morley, E.W. (1887). On the relative motion of the earth and the luminiferous ether. *American Journal of Science, 34*, 333–345.

Morton, J. (1969). Interaction of information in word recognition. *Psychological Review, 76*, 165–178.

Nagel, E. (1961). *The structure of science*, New York: Harcourt, Brace & World.

Nagel, T. (1974). What is it like to be a bat? *Philosophical Review, 83*, 435–450.

Peramunage, D., Blumstein, S.E., Myers, E.B., Goldrick, M., & Baese-Berk, M. (2010). Phonological neighborhood effects in spoken word production: An fMRI study. *Journal of Cognitive Neuroscience, 23*, 593–603.

Pinker, S., & Ullman, M. (2002). The past and future of the past tense. *Trends in Cognitive Science, 6*, 456–463.

Poincaré, H. (1952). *Science and hypothesis*. New York: Dover (Original English translation 1905).

Popper, K.R. (1945). *The open society and its enemies*. London: George Routledge.

Popper, K.R. (1959). *The logic of scientific discovery*. London: Hutchinson.

Pylyshyn, Z.W. (1973). What the mind's eye tells the mind's brain: A critique of mental imagery. *Psychological Bulletin, 80*, 1–25.

Pylyshyn, Z.W. (2002). Mental imagery: In search of a theory. *Behavioral and Brain Sciences, 25*, 157–182.

Quine, W.V.O. (1951). Two dogmas of empiricism. *Philosophical Review, 60*, 20–43.

Quine, W.V.O. (1953). *From a logical point of view*. Cambridge, MA: Harvard University Press.

Quinlan, P.T. (1991). *Connectionism and psychology*. Chicago: University of Chicago Press.

Rae, A.I.M. (1994). *Quantum physics: Illusion or reality?* Cambridge: Cambridge University Press.

Reed, S.K. (1974). Structural descriptions and the limitations of visual images. *Memory & Cognition, 2*, 319–336.

Rumelhart, D.E., McClelland, J.L., & the PDP Research Group. (1986). *Parallel distributed processing: Explorations in the microstructure of cognition* (Vol. 1). Cambridge, MA: MIT Press.

Russell, B. (1912). *The problems of philosophy*. Latest reprint Charleston, SC: BiblioLife (2008).

Russell, B. (1913). On the notion of cause. *Proceedings of the Aristotelean Society, 13*, 1–26.

Ryle, G. (1949). *The concept of mind*. Chicago: University of Chicago Press.

Salmon, W.C. (1998). *Causality and explanation*. Oxford: Oxford University Press.

Searle, J.R. (1979). What is an intentional state? *Mind, 88*, 74–92.

Searle, J.R. (1983). *Intentionality: An essay in the philosophy of mind*. Cambridge: Cambridge University Press.

Shepard, R.N. (1978). The mental image. *American Psychologist, 33*, 125–137.

Shepard, R.N., & Feng, C. (1972). A chronometric study of mental paper folding. *Cognitive Psychology*, 228–243.

Shepard, R.N., & Metzler, J. (1971). Mental rotation of three-dimensional objects. *Science, 171*, 701–703.

Simon, H. (1969). *The sciences of the artificial*. Cambridge, MA: MIT Press.

Skinner, B.F. (1947). Superstition in the pigeon. *Journal of Experimental Psychology, 38*, 168–172.

Skinner, B.F. (1950). Are theories of learning necessary? *Psychological Review, 57*, 193–216.

Skinner, B.F. (1969). *Contingencies of reinforcement: A theoretical analysis*. New York: Meredith Corporation.

Skinner, B.F. (1972). *Cumulative record* (3rd ed.). New York: Appleton-Century-Crofts.

Sklar, L. (1976). *Space, time, and spacetime*. Berkeley, CA: University of California Press.

Sober, E. (2002). What is the problem of simplicity? In A. Zellner, A.H. Keuzenkamp, & M. McAleer (Eds.), *Simplicity, inference and modelling: Keeping it sophisticatedly simple* (pp. 13–32). Cambridge: Cambridge University Press.

Sternberg, S. (1966). High-speed scanning in human memory. *Science, 153*, 652–654.

Sutherland, S. (1989). *The international dictionary of psychology*. New York: Continuum.

Swinburne, R. (2010). *Is there a god?* Oxford: Oxford University Press.

Tolman, E.C. (1948). Cognitive maps in rats and men. *Psychological Review, 55*, 189–208.

Toulmin, S. (1961). *Foresight and understanding*. New York: Harper & Row.

Wilton, R.N. (2016). Consciousness. Available by email from rnwilton@dundee.ac.uk or mcantram@yahoo.co.uk.

Wittgenstein, L. (1953). *Philosophical investigations* (trans. G.E. Anscombe). Reprinted Oxford: Blackwell Publishing (2001).

Zellner, A. (2002). Keep it sophisticatedly simple. In A. Zellner, H.A. Keuzenkamp, & M. McAleer (Eds.), *Simplicity, inference and modelling: Keeping it sophisticatedly simple* (pp. 242–263). Cambridge: Cambridge University Press.

Index

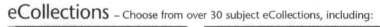